Iran and the

D0617693

Solving the Persian Puzzle

Edited by

Gideon Rose and Jonathan Tepperman

Foreign Affairs magazine is the leading forum for serious discussion of America's role in the world. It covers a broad range of topics related to U.S. foreign policy and international relations with a mix of non-partisan analysis, reportage, and reviews and criticism. It offers rigorous thinking by knowledgeable observers on important practical issues, presented in a style accessible to both professionals and a general audience. *Foreign Affairs* takes no institutional positions on policy issues and has no affiliation with the U.S. government. All views expressed in its publications and on its website are the sole responsibility of the author or authors.

Subscribe today at www.ForeignAffairs.com/subscribe.

For further information about *Foreign Affairs* or this publication, please write to *Foreign Affairs*, 58 East 68th Street, New York, NY 10065, or call Communications at 212.434.9888. Visit *Foreign Affairs*' website, www.ForeignAffairs.com.

Contents

The Roots of the Problem

Debating the Options

Contents

Other Voices

Contents

Introduction

Gideon Rose

August 22, 2012

FOR MORE than three decades, the Islamic Republic of Iran has posed a problem for the world. On the one hand, the Iranian regime's radical Islamist ideology, support for terrorism and regional subversion, and quest for an illegal nuclear weapons capability have made it a dangerous revisionist power determined to upend the existing regional and global order. On the other hand, Iran's position atop vast energy reserves and astride critical strategic choke points has made it an essential player in the global economy. This combination has produced a strange mixture of contention and connection, conflict and cooperation.

During much of this period, policymakers in Washington and other major capitals faced a dilemma. They felt they couldn't live with the Iranian regime, but that the world couldn't live without its oil. The result was often a rough and unacknowledged modus vivendi in which Iran's energy resources flowed onto global markets while the regime itself was pushed to the margins of international society. But recently this always tenuous compromise has grown even less stable. The Iranian nuclear program has moved forward, as have threats of an Israeli or American attack on it. And U.S. officials, having learned to live without Iranian energy, now want the rest of the world to do so as well. They have managed to wean Europe off it and are pressing China to follow. So each month

---

GIDEON ROSE is Editor of *Foreign Affairs*.

now seems to be billed as the one in which matters will finally come to a head, one way or another.

Foreign Affairs has been at the center of public debate on these issues from the beginning, publishing dozens of articles on all sides and facets of the subject, and so we've decided to respond to the current buzz by pulling together several of our most important pieces into one handy collection. We have focused squarely on the nuclear question, but have also included enough background and surrounding material to make the volume an excellent primer on Iran policy more generally. The authors include world-renowned experts from several disciplines and professional backgrounds, the arguments presented span every significant position on the political spectrum, and there are several Iranian and Israeli contributions to boot. The collection, in short, contains everything needed to understand the crisis over the Iranian bomb and develop an informed, independent opinion on what should be done about it.

The first section of the book contains three background articles that put the current debate in its proper historical and intellectual context. Gary Sick's 1987 essay, "Iran's Quest for Superpower Status," stresses the domestic political drivers of Iranian policy and argues that the main objective of Iranian leaders is to keep their theocratic regime in power. He also notes a curious and persistent pattern of Iranian behavior—"extreme rhetoric in public pronouncements balanced by calculated flexibility and utter realism in practice." Jahangir Amuzegar's 1997 essay, "Adjusting to Sanctions," explains why outsiders have always had a difficult time constructing an effective and nonporous sanctions regime that keeps Tehran in check. And Mohsen Milani's 2009 essay, "Tehran's Take," sets out the strategic logic behind Iranian policy today, showing how regime survival remains the dominant goal and what that means in practice.

The second section contains nine recent pieces laying out the pros and cons of various approaches to the Iranian nuclear problem.

Richard Haass' "Regime Change and Its Limits" provides an overview of the debate. Scott Sagan's "How to Keep the Bomb From Iran" counters what the author sees as a combination of "proliferation fatalism and deterrence optimism" and suggests a diplomatic approach. And Jacques Hymans' "Botching the Bomb" favors standing back and letting the natural problems that have afflicted nuclear weapons programs in other developing countries do their work in Iran as well.

Matthew Kroenig's "Time to Attack Iran" advocates taking the bull by the horns and launching a limited U.S. military strike at the Iranian nuclear program, setting it back several years if not permanently. Colin Kahl responds that it is "Not Time to Attack Iran," at least for now, since a military strike would cause more problems than it would solve. Instead, he favors continuing current U.S. policy. And in "Why Iran Should Get the Bomb," Kenneth Waltz pushes for permitting an Iranian nuclear capability as a way to balance the Israeli bomb and bring strategic stability to the broader Middle East.

James Lindsay and Ray Takeyh explore what would happen "After Iran Gets the Bomb," contending that such an outcome would mark a transition to a new and more complicated era of containment and deterrence. Suzanne Maloney criticizes what she considers "Obama's Counterproductive New Iran Sanctions," which do not offer a viable endgame for dealing with the current Iranian regime. And finally, Michael Ledeen, in "Tehran Takedown," pushes for a policy that makes even clearer the notion that regime change—support for a democratic revolution in Iran—is the central objective of U.S. strategy.

The third and last section of the book widens the discussion, bringing in voices from Iran and Israel. In "Sanctions Won't End Iran's Nuclear Program," Kayhan Barzegar presents a view of the conflict from Tehran's perspective, while in "How to Engage Iran," former Iranian official Hossein Mousavian lays out what he thinks went wrong in previous negotiations and what can be done to achieve better results now. Then Ronen Bergman explores "Netanyahu's Iranian Dilemma," Ariel Ilan Roth asks why Israel is so afraid of Iranian nukes, Ehud Eiran describes what would happen if Israel attacked Iran, and Dmitry Adamsky highlights Israel's own problematic nuclear policy, which seeks to deter without being deterred itself.

Reading over these arguments, one realizes how much better the authors are at criticizing others' favored approaches than they are at making bulletproof cases for their own chosen course of action. This reflects the dirty little secret of this debate (and so many others): All the options are lousy. The challenge is thus not picking a great course that delivers acceptable benefits at a reasonable cost and risk, but selecting a marginally less bad one with slightly fewer or less worrisome downsides than the others. Such a choice will depend not simply on one's substantive priorities and broad foreign policy orientation but also on one's risk tolerances, comfort with uncertainty, assessment of future political trends, and so forth. We would like to think that this collection provides the intellectual fuel to set such a deliberative process in motion.⚉

The Roots of the Problem

Iran's Quest for Superpower Status

Gary Sick

Foreign Affairs, Spring 1987

SINCE 1973 and the first oil shock, the center of gravity of Middle Eastern politics has been gradually shifting—from the eastern Mediterranean and the Arab-Israeli conflict toward the Persian Gulf and Iran. That process was accelerated in 1979 by the signing of the Egyptian-Israeli peace treaty, which dramatically reduced the likelihood of another Arab-Israeli war, and the nearly simultaneous climax of the Iranian revolution, which replaced the government of Shah Mohammad Reza Pahlavi with a radical theocratic regime under the leadership of Ayatollah Ruhollah Khomeini.

Iran has long harbored ambitions to become the superpower of the Persian Gulf. That prospect is not as improbable today as in the past. In recent years, despite the severe constraints imposed by a chaotic internal situation, Iran has managed a complex and dangerous set of international relationships with boldness, sangfroid and a considerable measure of success.

Americans are prone to evaluate developments in Tehran from the perspective of U.S. concerns, particularly after the revelation

GARY SICK is International Affairs Program Officer at the Ford Foundation responsible for activities relating to U.S. foreign policy. He was the principal White House aide for Iran during the Iranian revolution and the hostage crisis and is the author of *All Fall Down: America's Tragic Encounter with Iran*.

of U.S. arms sales. The world as seen from Tehran, however, constitutes sets of interlocking circles of threats and interests in which the United States is important but far from paramount.

The most important circle of attention is the constantly shifting balance of power within the revolution itself. Second, and only slightly less important, is the war with Iraq. Every aspect of the war has both practical and ideological implications for the survival of the regime; it is the object of the most intense controversy and debate. Third is oil policy—production, pricing and distribution—which is intimately associated with Iran's role in OPEC. For the most part, oil policy has not been a subject of political contention. Responsibility for management of the petroleum industry has been delegated to technicians who are essentially nonpolitical and nonideological. Iranian strategy in OPEC is apparently set by a small group of technocrats and political leaders at the very top of the power structure whose decisions, at least to date, have not been subject to serious public debate.

The fourth and fifth circles center on the two superpowers and their respective European allies, with the Soviet Union of more immediate and active concern than the United States. Sixth is Iran's relations with the regional states of the Persian Gulf and Middle East, including Syria and Libya. These two states occupy a special role as important (though not entirely reliable) allies in the Arab camp. Finally there is the collection of more distant states or entities, such as the United Nations, the Islamic Conference, the Nonaligned Movement, Japan, China, Vietnam and African states, that may be important to Iran on certain issues but tend to be marginal players in Iran's core concerns.

All of these circles overlap and interact. This analysis will focus on the domestic interests, which establish the baseline for all Iranian foreign policy behavior, including its war strategy; on relations with the two superpowers; and on Iran's relations with its regional neighbors.

THE ONE cardinal rule that the United States has learned— or should have learned—from its eight years of experience with revolutionary Iran, is that Iranian foreign policy is produced and conditioned by the hard imperatives of domestic politics in Tehran. The supreme goal of Ayatollah Khomeini and his associates is to assure the continuation of theocratic rule and to preserve the legitimacy of the new regime. They are playing for the highest of stakes— their own survival—a fact that focuses the mind wonderfully.

The first momentous encounter between the United States and the Islamic Republic of Iran—the seizure of the U.S. embassy in Tehran and the imprisonment of its occupants for 444 days—is best understood not in foreign policy terms but rather, as Khomeini designated it, as the "second Iranian revolution." The event was exploited by Khomeini to rid himself of troublesome secular elements within his own government and to mobilize mass support for a radical transformation of the political structure and leadership of the country. In retrospect, it is apparent that the rhythm of the hostage crisis was attributable more to internal developments in Tehran than to anything the United States and the international community did or did not do.

The original hostage crisis provided compelling evidence of a leadership prepared to take extraordinary international risks in pursuit of its own domestic agenda. Khomeini demonstrated a cool and calculated ability to manipulate events for his own benefit and to function purposefully in the midst of political and economic tumult. The leadership in Tehran also displayed an appreciation for damage limitation, as when it quietly squelched calls for a hostage trial and expelled a hostage who was seriously ill in order to avoid probable U.S. retaliation. Moreover, when the crisis had served its purpose and the institutions of a suitably theocratic government were firmly in place, Tehran negotiated the safe release of the hostages on terms that cost the regime dearly, relinquishing its original demands for a U.S. apology and return of the shah's assets.

In short, the leadership in Tehran showed itself to be exquisitely sensitive to its own internal priorities, immensely stubborn and tenacious in the face of nearly universal reproach, flexible and calculating in minimizing tactical damage to its own interests, and thoroughly pragmatic—even nonideological—when it determined that the game was no longer worth the candle.

There is perhaps no nation in the world that would be prepared to pay the very high price that Iran paid during the hostage crisis for its pursuit of idiosyncratic religio-revolutionary goals. Hence the perception of irrationality. But its actual performance was anything but irrational. On the contrary, Iran proved itself to be an adept and dangerous adversary, to be underestimated only at one's peril.

The Iranian revolution is now more than eight years old. During those years, the new theocratic regime has experienced a major confrontation with a superpower, six-and-a-half years of a brutal and devastating war with Iraq, a prolonged and ugly conflict with the Kurdish tribes in the northwest, several attempted coups, an open rebellion led by the Mujahedeen-al-Khalq in 1981, attempted subversion by the pro-Soviet Tudeh party, and a steady succession of bombings, assassinations, hijackings and other terrorist attacks. International sanctions and attacks on its oil production, refinery and export facilities have had a profound impact on the structure of its trade and finances.

At the same time, Iran has effected a near total overhaul of its political, economic and social institutions, from the national constitution down to the lowliest neighborhood committee. It has completely restructured the educational, judicial and social-welfare systems. In the midst of war, it has redesigned its military forces in a unique three-part structure composed of the traditional professional military, the parallel Islamic Revolutionary Guards Corps (commonly known as the *pasdaran*), and a massive levy of volunteers known as the *basij*. It has absorbed several million refugees from Afghanistan and the war fronts. The new regime has nationalized some 80 percent of the nation's industry, initiated a massive rural development program and engaged in a vociferous dispute about land reform.

Revolutionary Iran is a land of raucous debate where personal ambitions find expression in the vocabulary of revelation. Triumph over the old regime seems to have obliterated the past and convinced the new generation of revolutionaries that they could reinvent the world. That prospect released a remarkable surge of energy, but it also whetted immense appetites among those who hoped to define the future. Following the lead of Khomeini, who wove the rich symbolism of Shia Islam into the political fabric of the nation, personal and institutional rivalries are now conducted in the language, and with the same passionate conviction, reserved in medieval times for debate of first principles. Politics and metaphysics have fused.

Given the societal turmoil and the absolutist tenor of the debate, it is surprising that Iran has done as well as it has. The Iranian leaders have consolidated their control of the new revolutionary institutions. Their military forces, at great human expense, have reversed the early defeats of the war and have established a degree of momentum on the battlefield. They have continued to call on the long-suffering Iranian population for sacrifice, and the population—grumbling, to be sure, and with waning enthusiasm—has responded. They have demonstrated considerable skill and ingenuity in managing their oil industry in the face of Iraqi air raids. And despite eight years of seeming chaos, they have succeeded in paying off their entire foreign debt.

In fact, the pattern that has emerged in nearly every aspect of Iranian policy—foreign and domestic—has been extreme rhetoric in public pronouncements balanced by calculated flexibility and utter realism in practice, at least in those areas regarded as critical to survival. The war in particular has imposed a sense of realism and practical limitations.

III

INITIALLY, IRAN proclaimed its foreign policy in absolute, exclusionary terms in which Iran's role was to serve as the exemplar and catalyst to bring "Islam to the entire world." The Iranian Ministry of Foreign Affairs and the foreign service were purged repeatedly, and representatives abroad were exhorted to abjure traditional diplomacy in favor of revolutionary and doctrinal purity. Implicit in this approach was the assumption that the world was corrupt and, in the end, the world needed Iran more than Iran needed the world.

After four years of war that assumption was wearing thin. In October 1984, Khomeini summoned Iran's diplomatic representatives from abroad and instructed them to take a new approach:

> We should act as it was done in early Islam when the Prophet ... sent ambassadors to all parts of the world to establish proper relations. We cannot sit idly by saying we have nothing to do with governments. This is contrary to intellect and religious law. We should have relations with all governments with the exception of a few with which we have no relations at present. . . . We will not establish relations with America unless America behaves properly.

Iranian Prime Minister Mir Hossein Musavi-Khamenei expanded on these comments, noting that Iran had experienced difficulties in obtaining spare parts and military equipment because of U.S. pressures. He offered assurances to the nations of the region who had feared the export of Iran's revolution: "We do not want to export armed revolution to any country. That is a big lie. Our aim is to promote the Islamic Revolution through persuasion and by means of truth and courage. These are Islamic values."

These pronouncements marked a fundamental shift, not in Tehran's foreign policy goals but in its strategy for pursuing those goals. Khomeini and his lieutenants had discovered that a policy of unrelenting hostility and pressure was getting nowhere and, more important, was hampering Iran's ability to sustain itself at home while fighting a total war. This shift occurred at a moment when domestic popular discontent was on the rise due to shortages and inefficiencies. Moreover, the attempt to carry the war into Iraq appeared hopelessly bogged down, and domestic terrorist attacks were again becoming more frequent after a lapse of several years. It may also have been more than coincidental that this sharp reversal of policy was announced just as the United States was completing arrangements to reestablish diplomatic relations with Iraq, thus raising the prospect that both superpowers would be arrayed with Iran's mortal enemy.

The announcements in late 1984 were followed by a series of missions by key Iranian political figures to dozens of countries throughout the world. The message of these emissaries in each case was that Iran posed no military or subversive threat to its neighbors, that the war with Iraq was imposed on Iran by Saddam Hussein's aggression, that Iran had no territorial designs on Iraq or any other nation in the Persian Gulf region, and that Iran desired normal political and trade relations with all countries of the world.

The campaign had its setbacks; when President Hojatolislam Sayed Ali Khamenei visited Zimbabwe in January 1986 he created a diplomatic incident by refusing to attend a state dinner where wine was served and where a female cabinet minister was present. However, for the most part these delegations were successful in softening Iran's extremist image and in beginning to restore commercial and political ties that had been interrupted by the revolution. By mid-1986 Khomeini was able to assert: "There was a time when the situation was chaotic and everything was in ruins, but—thank God—everything is now proper and right. . . . Domestic and international affairs are put right."

Khomeini's claim was exaggerated, but his hyperbole was understandable in view of the considerable achievements of Iran's diplomatic offensive of the previous 18 months. Saudi Foreign Minister Saud al-Faisal had paid a formal visit to Tehran in May 1985, and Iran had agreed to help reduce tensions associated with the annual pilgrimage of large numbers of Iranians to Mecca. In return, Saudi Arabia reportedly agreed to provide regular shipments of refined petroleum products to Iran, whose refineries were under attack by Iraqi bombers. In February 1986 Iran had successfully crossed the Shatt al-Arab waterway, establishing a beachhead on Iraqi territory at Fao. Iran had also cemented new trade and diplomatic relations with China and a number of other countries.

Most important, when Khomeini made this statement he knew—as most of the rest of the world did not—that Iran had succeeded in restoring an arms supply relationship with the United States. By that time, Iran had received intelligence briefings from the United States on both Iraq and the Soviet Union and had taken delivery of some 1,500 TOW missiles and components for its U.S.-built Hawk air defense system. Only days before Khomeini's optimistic appraisal the United States had secretly dispatched former National Security Adviser Robert McFarlane to Tehran to urge Iran's assistance in freeing U.S. hostages in Lebanon and to seek a broader political dialogue with the Islamic revolutionary regime.

Iran understands as well as any country the implications of relative status implicit in diplomatic protocol. The fact that the United States was willing to send a high-level delegation to the capital of those who had kidnapped and held U.S. diplomatic hostages, to place itself in the hands of some of the very individuals who had participated in the hostage incident and to entreat them to reestablish a political relationship was perceived in Tehran as a remarkable vindication of their hard-line policy.

Khomeini later said that those hostile to Iran "have apparently come back today and presented themselves meekly and humbly at the door of the nation wishing to establish relations. . . . Right now, all big countries are competing to establish relations with Iran."

IV

REGRETTABLY, THERE is no evidence that the U.S. officials who planned the daredevil McFarlane mission had given any serious thought to the foreign policy signal it might convey. On the contrary, their decision to bring with them a chocolate cake inscribed with a small gold key suggests that the mission was regarded as an adventure, even a lark, and it betrays an embarrassing lack of understanding about the nature of the individuals with whom they were dealing.

The Iranians participating in contacts with the United States were engaged in a deadly gamble. They needed U.S. military equipment and spare parts, and they were prepared to do whatever was necessary to obtain them—including bargaining with the United States and (indirectly) even Israel. But powerful factions in Iran opposed any apparent softening of revolutionary resolve and continued to view any dealings with the "Great Satan" as treasonous. Perhaps that is what the speaker of the *Majlis* (parliament), Hojatolislam Hashemi Rafsanjani, had in mind when he made a public speech only one day after Khomeini's declaration that all had been "put right." Rafsanjani commented:

> There are at present two relatively powerful factions in our country with differences of view on how the country should be run and on the role of the government and that of the private sector in affairs. These two tendencies also exist in the Majlis, in the government, within the clergy, within the universities and across society as a whole. . . . They may in fact be regarded as two parties without names.

These two nameless parties, as suggested by Rafsanjani, are most prominently visible on domestic economic issues, e.g., land reform and nationalization. One faction, represented by such individuals as Minister of Heavy Industries Behzad Nabavi, favors government intervention in all major sectors of the economy. Another faction, reflecting the views of the traditional commercial interests of the bazaar and the conservative clergy, favors a deliberately free-market approach. Ayatollah Hussein Ali Montazeri, the designated successor to Khomeini, believes that "private enterprise proves to be a better administrator of business than is the government." If industry is privately owned, he has said "competition will be created and competition, supply and demand can solve many problems. However, if the government imports and hands the product over to the cooperative, the situation will remain as it is." These issues have been the subject of lively and well-publicized debate inside Iran ever since the fall of the shah.

Less publicity is accorded to debate on issues of military and foreign policy, so it is more difficult to identify members of different factions, to specify the precise nature of their differences and to judge the relative political influence of one party or another at any given moment. Nevertheless, questions about the appropriate division of labor between the regular military and the Revolutionary Guards have sparked fierce debates throughout the course of the war.

Khomeini has had to intervene repeatedly to legitimize the role of the Revolutionary Guards and their development into a mirror image of the regular armed forces, with their own naval and air arms as well as mechanized and armored units equipped with heavy weapons. These disputes have gone beyond questions of allocation of scarce military equipment to issues of basic strategy. The Revolutionary Guards have placed a high premium on personal zeal, in the use of both massive "human wave" assaults and small-unit guerrilla actions, with little regard for casualties. The professional military has argued for careful preparation and training, the development of adequate logistical support and a more deliberate approach designed to minimize casualties and the risk of defeat.

In early 1985 Rafsanjani announced that it was Iran's intent "to achieve victory with as few casualties as possible," suggesting that the professional military was being heeded. That impression was strengthened by the successful attack on the once busy port of Fao in early 1986. It was a complex amphibious operation, worthy of comparison to Anwar Sadat's surprise attack across the Suez Canal in 1973. The operation was prepared and rehearsed for an entire year, and it effectively blended the planning skills of the professionals with the courage and élan of the Revolutionary Guards.

By mid-1986, however, the rivalry—and the debate over strategy—had reemerged. In July, the commander of the Iranian ground forces, Colonel Ali Seyyed Shirazi, and the commander of the Revolutionary Guards, Mohsen Rezaie, clashed violently over policy. Khomeini called them to his residence on July 19, 1986, where he enjoined them to "seek unity." "You must endeavor," he told them, "not to think in terms of being members of the Armed Forces or those of the Guards Corps or of the Basij forces. . . . We must understand that if there were to be any disputes among you . . . not only are we doomed here and now, but we also are guilty before God." Both Shirazi and Rezaie were appointed members of the Supreme Defense Council, but three weeks later Shirazi was relieved of his post as commander of the ground forces, while Rezaie retained his operational command. It appeared that Shirazi had been kicked upstairs and that the Revolutionary Guard was once again in the ascendancy.

In October, Rafsanjani defined what he called "the new war strategy" of Iran in terms that sounded very much like a compromise. After the Fao operation he said, "the officials in charge of the war reached the conclusion that instead of utilizing diverse resources on an ad hoc basis, it is better to prepare for a concentrated program to carry out an extensive and destiny-making offensive, and it is necessary to carry out more extensive and sustained operations. . . . Our aim in all these movements is to reach our objectives through a huge movement, without shedding too much blood." This formula appeared to contain elements intended to accommodate the positions of both the military and the Revolutionary Guards. However, the series of offensives that Iran launched in late 1986 and early 1987 resulted in some of the highest casualty figures in the war to date.

v

THE MOST dramatic evidence of internal tension and dispute within the closed circle of Iran's foreign policy decision-makers was provided by the controversy surrounding contacts with the

United States. The internal opposition to the arms deal with Washington centered on a group of radical revolutionaries headed by Mehdi Hashemi. Hashemi, a relative by marriage of Ayatollah Montazeri, had long been associated with Montazeri's son, Mohammad, whose history of mental illness and radical behavior earned him the nickname of the "Red Sheikh" and eventually led the elder Montazeri to disassociate himself from his son's activities. Mohammad Montazeri died in a bombing incident in 1981 that killed more than 70 top leaders of the Islamic Republican Party.

Apparently Hashemi assumed direction of the Islamic Liberation Movement after the younger Montazeri died. Although the organization was formally disbanded in 1984, it retained close contact with hard-line elements in the Revolutionary Guards and continued to operate out of Ayatollah Montazeri's offices in Qom, trading on the Montazeri name. Hashemi had evidently learned of the McFarlane visit after the American visitors, left waiting at the airport, finally identified themselves to officials who turned out to be Revolutionary Guards. The Guards later attempted to kidnap McFarlane and his party, but were thwarted by forces loyal to Rafsanjani.

In August and September of 1986, Hashemi and his ultra radical supporters detected what they interpreted as evidence that Rafsanjani and others were softening their position on the war. Also, because of their close ties to radical Shia groups in Lebanon, they were no doubt aware of pressure being exerted to effect the release of U.S. hostages there. In early October, the Hashemi group circulated leaflets in Tehran opposing these policies and advocating resistance. Shortly thereafter, Hashemi and some 40 others were arrested, including several members of the Majlis. In retaliation, associates of Hashemi leaked to a Lebanese magazine details of the McFarlane visit to Tehran in May.

Thus the leak that put the entire U.S.-Iran relationship on the front pages of the world and initiated a crisis of confidence in the United States was the result of a power struggle inside Iran that was only indirectly concerned with the United States or even with foreign policy. This conclusion is strengthened by the extensive evidence provided in the Tower Commission report of February 26.

Members of the Majlis called for an investigation, and there were rare public demonstrations. Khomeini had to intervene personally to halt the escalating confrontation and to plead for unity. "What is wrong with you?" he asked the protesters. "I know some of you. . . . I do not want to break your heart, but you should not break the heart of the nation either. . . . You should not set up hard-liners and moderates. You should not create a schism." The protests promptly ceased, but the tensions between the "two parties without names" in Iran remained as fervent as ever.

This account suggests that the primary divisions within Iran relate to differences over the allocation of power on the domestic scene, not over foreign policy per se. The Hashemi group had been aware of the McFarlane visit since May and had tolerated it. It was only after Hashemi's arrest in October that they decided to use that information as ammunition against their internal opponents. The fundamental policy dispute centered not on the United States but on the continuing feud between the Revolutionary Guards and the regular military. That dispute goes to the heart of the meaning of the revolution, and it is certain to continue.

These events also suggest that the shorthand distinction between "radicals" and "moderates" inside Iran is at best misleading. If followed to its logical conclusion, it suggests that Khomeini—who was undoubtedly aware of the contact with the United States and who came to the defense of those who had arranged it—is a "moderate." It would be more accurate to say that there are powerful individuals among the Iranian leadership who are prepared to deal with the United States, if necessary, to preserve Iran's fundamental interests and to obtain military equipment and spare parts to prosecute the war with Iraq. Those individuals are not "pro-Western," but they are prepared to bargain with the West on secondary issues to promote the objectives of the revolution. Other individuals with close access to the power structure believe that the true purposes of the revolution can be served only by strict national self-reliance and rejection of any compromise or accommodation with the West.

The United States may be able to take advantage of this schism to pursue its own interests in the region, but it must do so with no illusions about the prospects of a fundamental shift in Iranian attitudes and with a skeptical awareness of the limits of maneuverability available to any Iranian political leader. Any approach to Iran should be undertaken with limited objectives and low expectations.

VI

THE EVOLUTION of Iran's relations with the Soviet Union is a fascinating example of jostling and cajoling by two utterly ruthless powers—one large, the other small—whose history as neighbors provides no basis for complacency or trust. The Iranian revolution surprised the Soviets nearly as much as the Americans. The Soviets, however, had less to lose and were quick to stitch together a strategy once they realized that the shah's regime was collapsing.

The leadership of the pro-Soviet Tudeh party returned to Iran in 1978 and 1979 from long exile in the U.S.S.R. and Eastern Europe and began rebuilding the party's strength. With Soviet assistance and support, the Tudeh adopted a policy of praising Khomeini and the revolution while calling for the establishment of a popular front in which they could participate in power. Initially Khomeini tolerated the Tudeh, and it looked as if its strategy of positioning itself inside the revolution might work. But the subterfuge was too blatant to be ignored. As one Islamic newspaper put it, the communists "threw a mouse in the soup of the revolution and, without any shame, shouted 'Oh hajji, we are also a partner.'" The Tudeh headquarters was occupied by *hezbollahi* ("partisans of God") in 1980, and by 1981 the party had been forced underground.

In early 1982, when Iran had pushed Iraqi troops back to the border and was considering its next move, the Soviets attempted to persuade Iran to accept a negotiated settlement of the war, warning that they would be obliged to resume major arms deliveries to Iraq if Iran tried to carry its counter-offensive into Iraqi territory. Iran rejected the Soviet threat and launched the first of its many attempts to break through Iraqi lines. The Soviets resumed arms deliveries, and by the end of the year Soviet-built missiles were falling on Dizful and other Iranian border cities.

During the last months of 1982 the Soviet vice consul in Tehran, Vladimir Kuzichkin, defected to British intelligence with documentary evidence about Soviet and Tudeh penetration activities in Iran. This information was fed back to authorities in Iran, who launched a concerted attack on the Tudeh infrastructure. In February 1983 the entire top leadership of the party was arrested, hundreds of Iranians were taken into custody, and 18 Soviet diplomats were summarily expelled from the Soviet embassy. Within a period of several months, much of the subterranean network that the Soviets had painstakingly developed in Iran was reduced to a shambles.

This exchange of blows established the pattern for Soviet-Iranian relations in the years that followed. The Soviets, discarding any illusions about collaboration with the Islamic revolution, withdrew their experts from steel and power projects begun under the shah, and they took off the gloves in their unofficial propaganda broadcasts. The so-called National Voice of Iran (NVOI), a clandestine radio station broadcasting in Persian from the vicinity of Baku in the Soviet Union, turned vitriolic:

> Every Iranian, be he fanatic or religious, can perceive the blood-stains of the Iranian nation's innocent children on the turban, cloak and garment of these clergymen who have seized power and on the ugly faces of these turbaned executioners. . . . We realize that our nation is confronting the bloodiest regime of all, which under the banner of religion . . . has surpassed all bloody fascist regimes. The Iranian people will never forgive them for these crimes. The day is not far off when the Iranian people will avenge the blood of their dear ones. . . . that historic day—the day of the nation's vengeance.

Iran subsequently arrested 60 ranking members of the pro-Soviet wing of the Fedayeen-al-Khalq in January 1986. Shortly thereafter Iran withdrew its ambassador to Moscow and placed him under arrest for suspected subversion. In September 1986 the Iranian navy for the first time stopped and searched a Soviet merchant vessel in the Strait of Hormuz.

Both sides were at pains, however, to keep this retaliatory cycle from getting out of hand. Even as they denounced each other, they were also carrying on a dialogue on issues of mutual importance. The Soviet Union was particularly anxious to restore deliveries of natural gas, which had been interrupted at the time of the revolution, and to avoid shoving Iran back into the arms of the United States.

An Iranian economic delegation visited the Soviet Union in September 1985. At about that time NVOI suspended its broadcasts, and the Soviet side agreed to resume supplying spare parts for the Soviet-built Isfahan power station. Iran, in turn, played a helpful role in securing the release of Soviet diplomats who were taken hostage in Lebanon in the same month and received a formal expression of gratitude from the Soviet ambassador.

Soviet First Deputy Foreign Minister Georgi Kornienko visited Tehran in February 1986 to pursue talks on natural gas and to establish an Aeroflot route between Tehran and Moscow. These contacts continued throughout 1986, resulting in the formal reestablishment of the Permanent Commission for Soviet-Iranian Economic Cooperation in December after a six-year lapse. Contrary to expectations, however, Iran refused to accept Soviet conditions for resumption of natural gas deliveries, and the Soviet economic delegation was treated to repeated public lectures about the Soviet presence in Afghanistan. It departed after signing a bland economic protocol that merely called for future meetings, and immediately after its departure mass rallies were organized throughout the country to protest the 1979 Soviet invasion. The subsequent visit of Iranian Foreign Minister Ali Akbar Velayati to Moscow in February 1987 kept the dialogue alive but otherwise left things very much as they were.

The absence of progress on the economic front may have been due in part to Soviet displeasure about Iran's arms deal with the United States and hints of Soviet involvement in the Hashemi affair. A Soviet diplomat in Tehran, Vyachel Solosin, was reported to have committed suicide on the same day that Hashemi was arrested, and shortly thereafter a clandestine Soviet station resumed propaganda attacks on the Iranian regime. Using the new name of "Radio of the Iran Toilers," it urged Iranians to "raise the call of long live peace, long live freedom, death to Khomeini, and death to U.S. imperialism." Rafsanjani responded by attacking Soviet arms deliveries to Iraq and denouncing Soviet pressures: "The Soviet Union is a powerful country and is very angry with us over Afghanistan. We say: 'Your troops are in Afghanistan, so this is how we will treat you.' We destroyed their elements, the Tudeh party, and we stood against their aggressive policies."

The Soviet Union and Iran, like the two proverbial scorpions in a bottle, are engaged in a wary and dangerous dance. Profoundly distrustful of each other yet bound together by geography, they circle and probe; but neither side is willing to risk pushing the situation to the limit. The two parties share a number of mutual interests, which they are prepared to pursue cautiously while keeping a watchful eye. The Soviets, however, make no secret of their preference for a more tractable partner than the religious ideologues now in power in Tehran, and in the event of a new outburst of political turmoil in Iran, the game could become deadly.

VII

THE SAME combination of toughness and tractability that Iran has adopted in its dealings with the United States and the Soviet Union has been employed in Tehran's relations with the conservative Arab governments of the Persian Gulf. The difference is that, unlike relations with the superpowers, Iran enjoys a preponderant power position in relation to its smaller neighbors. Iran controls half the coastline of the Gulf. Its total area is only slightly less than the area of all the other Gulf states combined. According to the latest Iranian census, more people have been born in Iran since the revolution (11 million) than the total number of citizens of all the other Gulf states combined.

The revolutionary regime in Tehran aspires, as did the shah before it, to be recognized as the dominant power of the region. Rafsanjani has characterized Iran's naval and other forces as "the guardians of Persian Gulf security," and has threatened to "turn off all the oil taps in the Persian Gulf" if Iran's oil exports are stopped. Iran has attacked shipping in the southern Gulf in retaliation for Iraqi air attacks on its shipping and as a warning to the Arab oil producers that their support for Iraq is not cost-free. Iranian fighter-bombers have also on occasion "accidentally" dropped bombs in Kuwaiti territory to underline Tehran's displeasure over Kuwaiti policies.

These heavy-handed tactics have been balanced, particularly in the past two years, by verbal assurances that Iran has "no covetous eye on Iraqi territory and it has high respect for the Persian Gulf littoral states." In recent years Iran has muted its public criticism of Saudi Arabia and the Gulf states, has welcomed a number of Gulf leaders to Tehran, and has maintained a continuing dialogue on issues relating to oil and the war through special emissaries and normal diplomatic channels.

The Gulf states have responded to these overtures and assurances with cautious reserve. They have reaffirmed their support for Iraq, but they also understand that if Iran prevails in its war with Iraq they will be left in a particularly vulnerable and exposed position, more dependent than ever on U.S. security guarantees.

Thus the news of U.S. arms supplies to Iran came as a considerable shock, for it suggested, at best, that the United States was insensitive to their security concerns or, at worst, that the United States had concluded that Iran was destined to win the war and was moving in advance to cement its ties with the victor. The fact that the U.S. policy was carried out in close cooperation with Israel only enhanced these suspicions.

The Gulf states have stoutly resisted being stampeded by Iran, but they are also realistic about the dangers of an emerging power imbalance in Iran's favor. Accordingly, they have hedged their bets by maintaining civil relations with Tehran and by accommodating Iranian policy on oil and other issues when they can do so without harm to their own basic interests. Iran seems to have accepted this situation as the best it can realistically achieve while it has its hands full with Iraq. If Iran should win a major military victory, or if the government of Saddam Hussein should collapse under Iranian pressure, Iran could be expected to be much more demanding of its smaller neighbors.

VIII

FROM THIS selective overview of Iran's efforts to deal with its foreign policy predicament, it is possible to draw a few general observations.

First, Iran's tactical performance has been shrewd and tough. The new regime has used whatever leverage available to seize the initiative and to keep its many adversaries off balance. The new leaders have been bold, but they have also been willing to bend their revolutionary principles when it suited their purpose. Iran's record as a middle-range power in dealing with two hostile superpowers and a host of smaller opponents is impressive.

Second, Iran has proved adept in the practice of "thump and talk" diplomacy, lashing out with what appears to be utter fearlessness and abandon at enemies of all sizes while simultaneously discussing agreements and concessions. Its reputation as a "crazy state" is deserved, but it is often not as crazy as it seems. President Nixon was not the first to recognize that a bit of perceived "craziness" can be valuable in keeping an opponent on the defensive. Iran exploited this attribute to the hilt with the Americans and Israelis in 1986 to get the maximum quantity of arms for the minimum number of hostages. The regime's repeated failure to keep its promises could always be explained by the craziness of the country's internal politics and of those holding the hostages in Lebanon. Whether true or contrived, it worked.

Third, it is apparent that Iran has modified, at least for the time being, its millenarian goal of bringing "Islam to the entire world" in favor of a policy that might be described as "clericalism in one country." Eight years after the revolution, Iran is less concerned with fomenting rebellion abroad and more concerned with consolidating and protecting the revolution within its own borders. That is not to say that Iran will not meddle abroad when the opportunity presents itself. It is doing so in Lebanon and probably elsewhere. It is also not to say that this is necessarily a permanent condition. It may be nothing more than a recognition that after more than six years of war Iran had best devote its limited resources to problems close to home. Nevertheless, it is a fact that the export of revolution does not get a great deal of attention in Tehran these days.

Perhaps because of the high price it paid for the original hostage crisis, Iran now attempts to avoid direct association with terrorism. Its deputy prime minister has declared (with a straight face) that it is "against hostage taking, which is also rejected by Islam" and that it will "take any measures in its power, wherever in the world" to oppose the taking of hostages. Obviously, Iran is willing to take advantage of its relationship with radical groups holding hostages for bargaining purposes, but in recent years it has attempted, with some success, to avoid leaving its own fingerprints on such operations.

Finally, it is apparent that Iran's determined drive to become the superpower of the Persian Gulf hinges, at least in the short term, on two unpredictable variables: Khomeini's health and the outcome of the war with Iraq. Over the past 24 months, Khomeini has had to intervene personally on at least three occasions to keep the internal situation from getting out of control. There is no one else who can play the crucial role of arbiter. It is unlikely that Iran will immediately unravel or undergo a dramatic transformation upon Khomeini's death, but its internal politics will become more volatile, the rivalries more intense and the outcomes less predictable.

Khomeini and those around him have gambled everything on the war—the economy, the nation's influence in international affairs, the legitimacy of the leadership, possibly the fate of the revolution itself. Each of these factors rises and falls as Iran seems to be winning or losing. If Iran is ultimately forced to accept an outcome approximating the status quo ante, it will be more likely to turn inward and focus on its enormous internal problems. However, a decisive Iranian victory would be interpreted as a vindication of extremist goals, and the relative moderation of Iran's recent performance would become a thing of the past.

In that event, the shift in the center of gravity would be complete. The Middle East could become polarized between two hostile regional superpowers—Israel in the west and Iran in the east—with dangerous and unpredictable consequences. Israel and the United States did not seem to give that possibility much attention in the past few years. It is time they did.❂

Adjusting to Sanctions

Jahangir Amuzegar

Foreign Affairs, May/June 1997

THE TOLL IN IRAN

THE AMERICAN-DRIVEN sanctions against Iran were meant to transform the "backlash state" into a law-abiding, cooperative, and constructive member of the world community. Washington expected trade and investment restrictions to cripple the productive base of the economy and curtail Iran's ability to support international terrorism or acquire sophisticated military hardware. Economic hardship and fiscal austerity would demoralize the population and turn it against the regime. And domestic popular discontent and external political isolation, Washington hoped, would bring the clerical leadership to its senses.

Inadequate hard data make an objective assessment of the sanctions difficult. Supporters of the policy claim that the cost to Iran has been immense, even greater than expected; critics dismiss the policy as self-defeating and divisive. What is certain, however, is that the economic, psychological, and political impact of the American sanctions has not produced the anticipated results or transformed the regime. Although the comparison may seem invidious, the Iranian economy under sanctions is in certain respects healthier and more stable than many developing

JAHANGIR AMUZEGAR, an international economic consultant, was Minister of Finance in Iran's pre-1979 government.

economies the United States has assisted. Militarily, Iran appears to be stronger now than in 1989, and is certainly less vulnerable than some U.S. allies in the region. The embargo has isolated Washington rather than Tehran.

Iranian officials concede that the boycotts have caused some economic "difficulties" but do not give details of their nature or magnitude. The affected areas, however, are not hard to identify. Finding non-U.S. buyers for Iranian oil and non-Americans to invest in Iran's offshore oil and gas fields has not been cost-free. Banned imports from the United States have been obtained through third parties at extra cost or substituted for from lower-quality sources. Replacing or renovating defense, industrial, and oil equipment based on American components has been more expensive or less satisfactory. Rescheduling of short-term arrears on debt to other countries has taken place under less favorable terms. Some foreign investors have shied away from lucrative projects in Iran under the threat of U.S. retaliation. Normal credits from international financial organizations have been delayed or canceled. Scheduled long-term foreign loans have been postponed. Foreign technological assistance in some sensitive areas has been withheld. Business confidence in Iran has been shaken, and the climate for foreign and domestic investment in the country has cooled.

There is no doubt that Iran would be in better shape had the United States not resolved to ostracize and cripple it. American economic and political pressures have hurt the Iranian economy, but they have not inflicted irreparable damage. Iran continues to produce its quota for oil set by the Organization of Petroleum Exporting Countries (OPEC), remains solvent, and maintains normal levels of trade and investment with the rest of the world. In fact, various international organizations and foreign media outlets report that economic indicators are healthier than at any time since the early 1990s. High surpluses have been registered in the current account, hard currency reserves are at record highs, and foreign debt payments are being made on schedule. Iran has had some success in raising medium- and long-term financing in Europe, the rial's official exchange rate has been kept stable, import cutbacks have slowed, and the Qeshm and Kish free trade zones have attracted some private foreign investment. Where sanctions were expected to be particularly damaging, their effect has been surprisingly benign. Daily crude oil production in 1996–97 was *higher* than in 1993–94. So were oil export receipts and net foreign assets. As a percentage of GDP, domestic investment was greater, and the budget deficit, external debt, and trade arrears smaller, after the sanctions, thanks in part to higher oil prices and appreciation of the U.S. dollar.

To be sure, the Iranian economy is not trouble-free. Inflation is unacceptably high. Unemployment and underemployment, particularly among the ever-growing numbers of graduates of the mushrooming diploma mills, combined with severe restrictions on normal social outlets for the youth, are economically debilitating and politically explosive. Cost and price distortions are enormous. Labor and capital productivity are low. There will be more turbulence ahead if the global oil market becomes depressed again. Yet American sanctions have not appreciably worsened any of these ills. And whatever their adverse effects, they have not been strong enough to induce a noticeable change in Tehran's behavior.

The psychological effects of the sanctions have been mixed. There are signs that despite their defiance of the United States, President Hashemi Rafsanjani and his government are wary of the costs of American enmity. They prefer compromise to confrontation and abhor the sanctions even as they claim immunity to them. As a sign of America's displeasure with the Tehran regime, the boycotts have also brought psychological comfort to discontented but passive groups inside Iran as well as the boisterous but ineffective opposition forces abroad, which both long for escalating American pressure that might lead to the eventual overthrow of the revolutionary regime.

On the other hand, U.S. sanctions have created a siege mentality; the regime's remaining supporters have become determined to rely on their own resources and ingenuity. The determination to become self-sufficient in most of their needs heralded a shift to other sources of equipment for exporting oil and stronger ties with Asia, Africa, and Latin America. The kinds of sophisticated goods and services now designed and produced in Iran—increasingly for export abroad—did not exist ten or even five years ago. Supreme Leader Ayatollah Sayed Ali Khamenei has publicly welcomed the U.S. ban as a boon to popular mobilization and self-reliance.

The political impact of U.S. pressure has, if anything, also worked in Tehran's favor. When the United States first imposed sanctions on Iran in the mid-1980s, the Islamic Republic's loyal friends around the world could be counted on one hand. In the mid-1990s, the regime's declared enemies were only two: the United States and Israel. Despite the sanctions—or perhaps because of them—Tehran now has close ties to Russia, China, India, Indonesia, and Brazil, which together account for nearly half the world's population. Relations with most countries in Asia and Africa are friendly, and with the European Community they are businesslike, despite recurrent verbal duels concerning Salman Rushdie and other high-profile human rights cases. There are hundreds of treaties of friendship, cooperation, trade, and cultural exchange with both developing and developed countries on six continents. A regime that some American high officials have called an "outlaw state" has been invited to lend its good offices to resolving disputes between Azerbaijan and Armenia, Sudan and Uganda, and other sovereign nations. Tehran has also been active in mediating between ethnic factions in Afghanistan, Tajikistan, Iraq, Bosnia, and elsewhere. Islamic government representatives have won important committee seats in the United Nations and its affiliate organizations in spite of Washington's objections. Last December the International Court of Justice in The Hague voted 14 to 2 to reject Washington's plea for dismissal and to hear Tehran's case against the United States for the deliberate destruction of three Iranian offshore oil platforms in the Persian Gulf in 1987. The Tehran government now feels confident enough about its economy to consider membership in the World Trade Organization.

The Islamic Republic still has festering quarrels with Iraq and is embroiled in political conflicts with Algeria, Bahrain, Egypt, Saudi Arabia, the United Arab Emirates, and the Taliban in Afghanistan. Relations with the U.N. Human Rights Commission are also tense; Maurice Copithorne may join Reynaldo Galindo Pol as the second U.N. rapporteur to be declared persona non grata in Iran because of reports critical of the country's human rights record. Nevertheless, its "isolation index" is now the lowest since the revolution.

WHY THE SETBACKS?

THE REASONS for the evident lack of success of Washington's containment policy are not difficult to fathom. Historically, economic sanctions have worked only when they have been universal and comprehensive, consistent and credible—in short, leakproof. In this case, none of those conditions has held.

Except with respect to transfers of sophisticated military weapons, the American policy toward Iran has been essentially unilateral. Since 1993, and culminating in the Group of Seven Halifax summit in June 1995 and the Sharm al-Sheikh antiterrorism summit in March 1996, Washington has tried and failed to enlist its major allies in its campaign against Iran. Reactions to American initiatives have been negative or, at best, noncommittal. The allies regard the U.S. stance of ignoring Iran's legitimate role in the region as unrealistic and the sanctions' uncompromising message of "redeem yourself or be damned" a nonstarter. Defying the U.S. secondary boycott legislation under the Iran and Libya Sanctions Act of 1996, the European Union has lodged a formal complaint with the World Trade Organization and even warned Washington of retaliatory measures if it tries to act under the law. American allies like Turkey, Kuwait, and the United Arab Emirates have now expanded commercial links with Iran. Oil and natural gas deals with the countries of the Commonwealth of Independent States have proceeded as planned. Japan, Russia, China, Canada, and others have largely ignored American requests for trade sanctions. Only Israel and a wavering Uzbekistan have answered Washington's call.

American allies may have their own ulterior motives for opposing the containment strategy—desires to safeguard their historical ties with Iran, expand their commercial interests in a lucrative market, or simply assert their political independence from Washington. But their reservations reflect a second flaw of U.S. sanctions: inconsistency, which saps their credibility. The sanctions have sometimes been selective and arbitrary in their targets, and the United States has frequently breached the policy when it suited its interests. Syria has been on the same list of "terrorist states" as Iran, yet high U.S. officials have often courted Damascus. Sudan and Iran were both barred by the Antiterrorist Act of April 1996 from engaging in any financial transactions with U.S. companies; yet Occidental Petroleum was granted a special exemption to enter into a major oil deal with the Khartoum government soon after the bill was signed. On nuclear weapons, North Korea has pursued a development program similar to Iran's, yet Iran has been denied the same right accorded to Pyongyang, under the Nuclear Nonproliferation Treaty, to develop peaceful uses of nuclear energy. On human rights, China and some U.S. friends in the Middle East—Egypt, Pakistan, Saudi Arabia, and Turkey—have been cited by the State Department as some of the world's worst violators, yet they have enjoyed thriving trade and normal diplomatic relations with the United States. Finally, Washington bitterly declared secondary boycotts to be illegal when the Arab League applied them to Israel, but it now urges its partners to honor them against Iran.

The containment policy has also lacked credibility because of Washington's repeated departures from stated principles. The secret arms deal with Tehran during President Reagan's administration, an aborted attempt at diplomatic rapprochement under President Bush during the release of American hostages in Lebanon in 1991, and the decision under President Clinton to allow Iran to send clandestine arms shipments to Bosnia are flagrant examples. Furthermore, until 1995, the U.S. embargo applied only to a handful of dual-use items and conspicuously excluded oil. Thus, while Washington was exhorting its allies to stop trading with Iran, the United States had become Iran's fourth-largest trading partner.

The final reason U.S. sanctions have been ineffective is that they have not been airtight. Companies and contractors from other Western countries have served as proxies for U.S. subsidiaries abroad. Countries that were not even among the top 25 nations trading with Iran prior to the sanctions now rank fifth and sixth. Shops in Iran are stocked with American goods of every description—many smuggled in, but others imported legally through neighboring countries. Some Iranian exports also have found their way into the American market through third parties and legal loopholes.

WILL TEHRAN CRY UNCLE?

SANCTIONS MATTER not because they can, in their present configuration, bring the Islamic regime to its knees, but because they may handicap it in the race to rapid economic growth. The current U.S. policy is likely to remain largely ineffective, if not counterproductive, unless it is backed by a U.N. Security Council resolution specifically banning exports of oil from Iran and gaining the compliance of all major petroleum-importing countries. Without oil revenues, Iran's economy would quickly be paralyzed. However, judging from the European Union's reaction to the U.S. secondary boycott law—the one issue, incidentally, on which the EU membership has unanimously agreed—and given the fierce opposition that Russia, France, and China would likely raise in the Security Council, no such resolution is in sight at the United

Nations. Furthermore, an embargo against Iranian oil would likely push crude prices through the roof for a while, another reason all oil-importing nations would resist it. Washington, therefore, may have to go it alone unless its allies and the world community are presented with irrefutable evidence of Tehran's direct involvement in a dastardly terrorist act, such as the June 1996 truck bombing of a housing complex in Dhahran that took the lives of 19 American military personnel. For its part, Iran can live with U.S. sanctions for a long time with much less difficulty than Cuba or Vietnam, although it cannot prosper without Washington's blessing.

In dealing with the Tehran regime Washington has four distinct, and familiar, policy options. At one end of the spectrum, it can discontinue sanctions and follow the easy route of "silence tinged with indifference or disdain," as an old U.S. intelligence hand has suggested. But while attractive, such a policy may be neither practical nor prudent; Iran's multifaceted activities and machinations in the region cannot be ignored, and the regime may not go out without a bang. At the other extreme, Washington may choose a military confrontation with Tehran, as anti-Iran hawks advocate, to roll back the regime. But this option is fraught with incalculable risks, would be internationally insupportable if launched without clear provocation, and would probably be domestically unpopular, particularly if it involved U.S. troop deployments and American casualties.

The third choice is to tighten comprehensive unilateral sanctions. Persistent advocates of the U.S. boycott still argue that Iran is currently weak and vulnerable economically and financially, that it needs a bailout from the West in the form of credits, technology, and management, and that sanctions will work most effectively if other major industrial powers follow— but even unilateral American sanctions can make a big difference. Patience and perseverance are all that is needed.

Assuming this assessment is correct, the get-tough policy is still not risk-free. Enhanced U.S. sanctions may hasten the day of reckoning, but they run the risk of arousing formidable nationalist resistance in Iran. Serious imbalances and deficiencies plaguing the Iranian economy pose a latent threat to the regime's survival because they give rise to sociopolitical tensions that weaken the rulers' grip on power. With or without the U.S. embargo, the regime is likely to implode eventually unless there is a dramatic change in its domestic Islamic rule and its anti-Western worldview. Therein lies the reason for the regime's survival somewhat beyond its time: not in spite of sanctions, but because of them.

Already sensing a general anxiety across the land about further U.S. economic pressure, the clerical leadership, in a series of smart public relations maneuvers, has blamed the country's economic shortcomings and setbacks on undisguised American hostility toward Islamic rule. Washington's frequent demonization of the government in Tehran has been seized on to demonstrate Iran's unique importance as the defender of the faith and supporter of the oppressed against an arrogant superpower. Taking advantage of the Shiites' historical glorification of martyrdom, the leadership portrays Iran as the victim of a cruel and hostile hegemon. The sanctions themselves are shrugged off as insignificant, but they are highlighted as proof of American hostility.

The regime's appeal to Iranian nationalism, particularly the clever hints that enhanced U.S. sanctions and continued hostility threaten Iran's sovereignty and territorial integrity, has been an effective ploy. Not a single group in the vast array of current opposition to the Islamic government, no matter how hostile to theocratic rule—including die-hard monarchists—wants to see sanctions topple the regime if that means Iran's Balkanization. On no other issue have the disparate groups been so united for so long.

The remaining option is to seek a prudent modus vivendi with the rogue state. The regime is a religious oligarchy related by blood and financial ties to the bazaar merchant class. Bazaaris' passion is not policy, but profit. For their partners in the leadership, the overarching goal is not ideological rigor but power. Ayatollah Khomeini in 1988 ingloriously accepted the cease-fire in the eight-year war with Iraq that he had vowed to pursue to total victory. His sole motive was to preserve Islamic rule and keep the clergy in power. Any proposal that could strengthen the economy and give the regime a better chance of survival is likely to get a positive response. The reason that this option, despite its many advocates within the foreign policy establishments on both sides of the Atlantic, has not been actively pursued is because its supporters are looked upon as accommodationsists, appeasers, or opportunists. In neither country is the leadership anxious to take the initiative for fear of being labeled sellouts by the opposition.

SHARED INTERESTS

THE OUTSTANDING differences on many matters of legitimate national concern—including each country's self-proclaimed manifest destiny (Iran to propagate Islam, America to promote democracy)—may rule out relations of the sort that prevailed between Iran and the United States before 1979. But they cannot mask the significant interests that the two *countries*—as distinct from their *governments*—still share. In spite of mutual assertions to the contrary, regional instability, chaos, and tension are in neither country's political or economic interest. Both countries have a vital interest in the free flow of oil through the Persian Gulf and the avoidance of maritime incidents. Both need each other geopolitically, as the twin pillars of a regional counterbalance to Russia's potentially expansionist aspirations within the Commonwealth of Independent States and toward the warm waters of the Persian Gulf. And, finally, both countries can fruitfully cooperate in developing and transporting the energy resources of the Central Asian states and the Caucasus, reducing those nations' dependence on Russia.

For the moment, these mutual interests may not seem impressive to Washington. After the breakup of the Soviet Union, the defeat of Saddam Hussein and Iraq, and the increase in the supply of non-OPEC oil, Iran may have lost its geostrategic, military, and economic cachet for the United States. Washington may perceive no need to make concessions to establish a dialogue with Tehran, hoping instead to force the regime's hand through comprehensive new sanctions. But the current phase may be transitory. Before long the Russian Federation may again be a superpower, and a post-Saddam Iraq may be just as menacing to its neighbors. Iran, regardless of its governing regime, will remain the Middle East's most populous and second-largest country, surrounded by 15 neighbors with which it shares land borders or bodies of water, a major global energy source with 10 percent of the world's oil and 15 percent of its natural gas, a pivotal player both in the region and within OPEC, and a gateway to Central Asia. In a region where national interests are increasingly defined in terms of shifting national alliances and coalitions, a strong, integral Iran may be sorely needed as a constructive force if there is to be stability and progress. The ultimate effects of the U.S. containment policy must be regarded in that light.

Assuming that Iran's territorial integrity and political independence are in the United States' own long-term national interests, a change in the containment policy may be a reasonable insurance premium. Washington may wish to reactivate the long-standing offer of a dialogue between duly authorized representatives, in a confidential manner, without preconditions. Should this option be chosen, a strategic reassessment would be in order. To be effective and credible, the dialogue must avoid going into a long wish list of expected changes in bilateral behavior and instead single out one or two issues of crucial importance to both parties, such as nuclear proliferation, the Arab-Israeli peace process, and the U.S. military presence in the Persian Gulf. The United States should give the Islamic Republic some reasonable incentives for cooperation, such as the release of frozen assets or new loans from the World Bank, and clear disincentives for intransigence, including intensified political pressure or even more drastic action. Under this policy of *reciprocal response*, each offending behavior may be dealt with through quid pro quo, without bestowing a seal of approval on or resorting to a blanket condemnation of either party's overall position.

Should Washington decide that its containment policy is the right course and Tehran continue its anti-American belligerence, the current stalemate will continue. Without a strong consensus among U.S. allies and a tacit understanding with Russia and China not to help Iran, and without convincing the regime's opponents that Iran's territorial integrity will not be jeopardized by U.S. sanctions—that the end of the Islamic Republic will not be the end of Iran—the boycott might still not reach its goal by the year 2010 or even 2020, if the Chinese, Vietnamese, and Cuban experiences serve as precedents.✑

Tehran's Take

Understanding Iran's U.S. Policy

Mohsen M. Milani

Foreign Affairs, July/August 2009

ALTHOUGH A great deal has been written about the United States' policy toward Iran, hardly anything comprehensive has been produced about Iran's policy toward the United States. Given Washington's concerns that the United States faces "no greater challenge from a single country than from Iran," as the 2006 National Security Strategy put it, this lack of serious attention is astonishing. What does exist is sensationalistic coverage about Iran's nuclear ambitions and about mad mullahs driven by apocalyptic delusions and a martyr complex. That picture suggests that Iran's policy consists of a series of random hit-and-run assaults on U.S. interests and that its leaders, being irrational and undeterrable, must be eliminated by force.

In fact, Tehran's foreign policy has its own strategic logic. Formulated not by mad mullahs but by calculating ayatollahs, it is based on Iran's ambitions and Tehran's perception of what threatens them. Tehran's top priority is the survival of the Islamic Republic as it exists now. Tehran views the United States as an existential threat and to counter it has devised a strategy that rests on both deterrence and competition in the Middle East.

MOHSEN M. MILANI is Professor of Politics and Chair of the Department of Government and International Affairs at the University of South Florida in Tampa.

To deter any possible military actions by the United States and its allies, Iran is improving its retaliatory capabilities by developing the means to pursue asymmetric, low-intensity warfare, both inside and outside the country; modernizing its weapons; building indigenous missile and antimissile systems; and developing a nuclear program while cultivating doubts about its exact capability. And to neutralize the United States' attempts to contain it, the Iranian government is both undermining U.S. interests and increasing its own power in the vast region that stretches from the Levant and the Persian Gulf to the Caucasus and Central Asia. Although it is being careful to avoid a military confrontation with the United States, Tehran is maneuvering to prevent Washington from leading a united front against it and strategically using Iran's oil and gas resources to reward its friends.

Iranian foreign policy today is as U.S.-centric as it was before the 1979 revolution. Mohammad Reza Shah Pahlavi relied on Washington to secure and expand his power; today, the Islamic Republic exploits anti-Americanism to do the same. Policy has been consistent over the years partly because it is determined by the supreme leader, who is also the commander of the security and armed forces and serves for life. Iran's defiance has in some ways undermined the country's national interests, but it has paid huge dividends to the ruling ayatollahs and helped them survive three tumultuous decades in power.

Today, Ayatollah Sayyid Ali Khamenei is the supreme leader, and he makes all the key policy decisions, usually after Iran's major centers of power, including the presidency, have reached a consensus. This means that the outcome of the presidential election in June will have some, although probably limited, ramifications for Iran's foreign policy. President Mahmoud Ahmadinejad and his two major reformist rivals, Mir Hossein Mousavi and Mehdi Karroubi, have all supported engaging in negotiations with Washington—a political taboo just a few years ago. Ahmadinejad would be less likely to compromise than his more moderate competitors, but, thanks to the support he has among major anti-American constituencies inside and outside the Iranian government, he would be in a better position to institutionalize any shift in policy. Although Iran's president can change tactical aspects of the country's foreign policy, he cannot single-handedly alter its essence. Only Khamenei, the ultimate decider, can do that. And he will do that only if a fundamental change in policy would not undermine his own authority and if it enjoys broad support from among the major centers of power.

THE HUNGRY WOLF AND THE FAT SHEEP

THE ROOTS of anti-Americanism in Iran—really, an opposition to U.S. policies—can be traced to the 1953 coup against Mohammad Mosaddeq, which was backed by the CIA and MI6. Anti-American sentiment was strengthened when in 1964 Ayatollah Ruhollah Khomeini, who would become Iran's first supreme leader after the revolution, opposed a treaty granting legal immunity to U.S. military advisers in Iran and declared that Iran had become a "U.S. colony." By 1979, the revolutionaries were portraying the Iranian monarch as "America's shah" and had made "independence" a defining slogan of their movement. After the taking of hostages at the U.S. embassy in Tehran that year, anti-Americanism became an enduring feature of the state's Islamic ideology. Since then, Iran's leaders have deftly linked the survival of the Islamic Revolution to Iran's independence, depicting the United States as antithetical to both. No one has drawn this link more vividly than Khomeini: he called the United States "the great Satan" and compared U.S. relations with Iran to those between a hungry wolf and a fat sheep. As hostility between the two states intensified, a Manichaean security paradigm developed in both of them. Each one came to perceive the other as a mortal enemy in a zero-sum game. Anti-Americanism and anti-Iranian feelings became two sides of the same coin.

For decades, the Iranian regime has used anti-Americanism to crush its opponents at home and expand its power abroad. After

1979, documents selectively released by the radical students who occupied the U.S. embassy were invoked to establish links between opponents of the Islamic Republic and the U.S. government. Hundreds of people were consequently defamed, jailed, or exiled. In the 1980s, when the young regime was simultaneously struggling to consolidate its rule and fighting a war with Iraq, allegations that the U.S. government was attempting to stage coups in Tehran and prevent Iran from winning the war strengthened the sentiment.

Over time, anti-American constituencies in Iran have proliferated and gained ground in various institutions. Some of them oppose the United States for purely ideological reasons. Others have substantial economic interests in preventing the normalization of relations between Tehran and Washington: they profit from domestic black markets and international trade routes established to bypass U.S. sanctions. Moreover, the foreign organizations that Iran supports throughout the Middle East, and that Washington considers to be terrorist groups, have created effective lobbies in Iran that thrive on this animosity.

Yet now, as under Khomeini, the intensity of the anti-Americanism prevailing in Iran is ultimately determined by the supreme leader. As president, Khamenei declared in 1981, "We are not like [Salvador] Allende [a Chilean president ousted by a coup allegedly backed by Washington], liberals willing to be snuffed out by the CIA." Today, Khamenei still considers the United States to be an existential threat. Washington surrounds Iran with bases in Bahrain, Kuwait, and Qatar and massive troop buildups in Afghanistan and Iraq. It makes friends with the leaders of Iran's neighbors. And its nuclear-equipped naval carriers patrol the Persian Gulf. Khamenei sees the United States as isolating Iran, strangling it with economic sanctions, sabotaging its nuclear program, and beating the drums of preemptive war. He thinks Washington is pursuing regime change in Tehran by funding his opponents, inciting strife among Iran's ethnic minorities, and supporting separatist organizations such as the Baluchistan-based Sunni insurgent group Jundallah, which has killed scores of Revolutionary Guard members.

PREFER TO DETER

TEHRAN HAS responded to Washington's policy of containment with a strategy of deterrence. Tehran first developed this strategy against Iraq after Iraq invaded Iran in September 1980 and then, as the 1980s unwound and the menace of Iraq faded, redirected it toward the United States. Today, this approach is the result both of Iran's perception of its vulnerabilities and of the constraints that the international community has imposed on the country.

Iran's deterrence strategy has four components. The first is developing the means to fight an asymmetric, low-intensity war, inside and outside the country. In recent years, particularly after U.S. troops arrived in Afghanistan and Iraq, the Revolutionary Guards have played an increasingly important role in maintaining internal order. They have also improved Iran's retaliatory capability in case of an invasion or surgical strikes against its nuclear facilities or the headquarters of its security forces. Khamenei's recent decision to decentralize the command-and-control structure of the Revolutionary Guards serves this purpose. So do the alleged ability of Iran's troops to transform themselves into nonconventional forces within days and Iran's thousands of small Iranian-made assault boats, which could create havoc for the U.S. Navy, as well as its thousands of motorcycles equipped with light artillery, which could impede the advances of an invading army. Iran's support for terrorist actions against U.S. interests in the Middle East is part and parcel of its strategy of asymmetric warfare. For example, in 1983, during the civil war in Lebanon, a group associated with the Iranian-backed Hezbollah killed 220 U.S. marines.

The modernization of Iran's weapons systems is the second component of its deterrence strategy. Decades of arms embargoes from the West have left Iran with limited access to advanced weapons, and Iran has consequently purchased relatively small arms supplies. Between 2002 and 2006, it spent $31 billion on military purchases, compared with $109 billion for Saudi Arabia and a total of $48 billion for Bahrain, Kuwait, Oman, and the

United Arab Emirates—four states with a combined population smaller than that of the city of Tehran. The embargoes have also caused an indigenous military-industrial complex to develop, controlled and financed by the state. It employs thousands of people and is connected to the country's major universities and think tanks. Most important, it is in charge of research and development for Iran's missile and nuclear technologies.

Developing indigenous missile and antimissile systems is the third leg of Iran's deterrence strategy. Tehran began building missiles during the Iran-Iraq War and accelerated its program after the "war of cities," in 1988, when both states showered the other's cities with missiles. Iran has used technical support from China and Russia to to develop its missile technology. Now, it manufactures its own missiles and claims that two types, the Shahab and the Ghadr, can reach Israel. These missiles are known for their inaccuracy and limited offensive application. But they give Iran the power to retaliate against attacks, particularly in the Persian Gulf, where it could readily upset international navigation.

The fourth component of Iran's deterrence strategy is its nuclear program. The Iranian government claims that its program is designed for peaceful purposes—using nuclear weapons would violate Islamic law, it says—but Washington (and much of the West) accuses it of having a secret program to build the bomb. So far, the International Atomic Energy Agency has found no smoking gun or any evidence that Iran has diverted its nuclear program toward military purposes. But nor has it been able to confirm Tehran's peaceful intentions, because the Iranian government has refused to answer some major questions. Now that Iran has joined a small club of countries that can enrich uranium to a low level of purity, it seems unlikely to cave in to international pressure and accept zero enrichment in the future.

Why, given all the sanctions imposed by the United Nations, does Iran not cry uncle and stop its nuclear program? For one thing, by insisting that its nuclear project is essential for the country's domestic energy needs and scientific development, Tehran has effectively turned U.S. opposition to its program into a nationalist cause, pointing to it as proof that Washington intends to hold Iran back. (In an attempt to awaken national pride, the government has had the atom symbol printed on 50,000 rial bills.) For another, the nuclear impasse creates an excellent bargaining chip for Tehran in future negotiations. This may be the reason that Iran's leaders are cultivating uncertainty about the country's actual capability. It does appear, however, that they have decided to develop the infrastructure to build the bomb but not yet the bomb itself. (Former President Ali Akbar Hashemi Rafsanjani claimed in 2005, "We possess nuclear technology that is not operationalized yet. Any time we decide to weaponize it, we can do so rather quickly.") Iran and the United States seem to be engaged in a game of poker, with Tehran not showing its cards about its nuclear capabilities and Washington refusing to exclude the possibility of attacking Iran. Washington has the better hand, but the better hand does not always win.

COUNTERCONTAINMENT

FOR THREE decades, the United States has sought to contain Iran and has imposed on it a variety of sanctions in an effort to do so. To try to neutralize these measures' effects, Iranian leaders have played major powers off against one another, forged alliances of convenience, and asserted Iran's interests at the regional and global levels.

First, Iran has tried to create a wedge between the United States and the United States' European allies. Iran's leaders believe that increased trade with the European Union will allow them to exploit differences among the organization's 27 members and discourage it from supporting regime change in Tehran, the total containment of Iran, or a military attack. In other words, they see the EU as a potential counterweight to the United States. After Iran restarted its uranium-enrichment activities in 2003, the EU ended its "constructive engagement" policy and imposed limited sanctions on Iran to tame its nuclear ambitions. Although these restrictions have prevented both Iran from gaining access to advanced technologies and European firms from making substantial investments in Iran, they have had a negligible impact on the overall volume of trade. The EU remains Iran's leading trading partner, accounting for about 24 percent of Iran's total international trade: the EU's total imports from Iran (mostly energy) increased from 6.3 billion euros in 2003 to 12.6 billion euros in 2007, and its exports to Iran (mostly machinery) remained the same, at about 11.2 billion euros, during that period. On the other hand, the fact that France, Germany, and the United Kingdom supported the referral of Iran's case from the International Atomic Energy Agency to the UN Security Council in 2005 proved the limits of Iran's wedge policy. The move, which highlighted the determination of the major Western powers to tame Iran's nuclear ambitions, was a major defeat for Tehran and a major victory for Washington.

The second component of Iran's strategy to undermine the United States' containment measures is to move closer to states that could counterbalance the United States. Iran has signed major economic and military agreements with China and Russia. It sees these two countries as natural allies, since they oppose the United States' unilateralism and its efforts to isolate Iran and have only reluctantly backed the sanctions against Iran. But the fact that they have supported the UN sanctions at all has proved to Tehran that when pressed, Beijing and Moscow are more likely to gravitate toward Washington than toward Tehran. Russia has not yet finished building the Bushehr nuclear reactor, which it had committed to completing by 2006, and Moscow may be willing to pressure Tehran to change its nuclear policies if the Obama administration decides not to build antimissile systems in Russia's neighborhood.

But Iran continues its efforts. With little alternative but to rely on China and Russia as counterweights to the United States, it recently asked to upgrade its status in the Shanghai Cooperation Organization, a six-party security organization that includes

China and Russia, from observer to full member so that it would receive assistance from other members if it were ever attacked. It has also become much more active in trying to popularize anti-Americanism within the Nonaligned Movement and the Organization of the Islamic Conference, and it has solidified its ties with Washington's most vocal opponents in the United States' backyard: Bolivia, Cuba, Ecuador, Nicaragua, and Venezuela.

The third facet of Iran's countercontainment strategy is to use its energy resources to reward its allies. No country in the region is as well endowed with energy resources as Iran is, not even Saudi Arabia: Iran's oil reserves total about 138.4 billion barrels, and its natural gas reserves total about 26.5 trillion cubic meters. (Although Saudi Arabia's oil reserves, which total approximately 267 billion barrels, are larger than Iran's, its natural gas reserves, which total about 7.2 trillion cubic meters, are much smaller.) Oil diplomacy has long been a strategy of Tehran's, of course. During the Rafsanjani presidency, it briefly served as a means to start normalizing relations with Washington. In that spirit, Iran signed in early 1995 a $1 billion oil deal with the U.S. energy company Conoco, the largest contract of its kind since 1979. But the deal was soon terminated when, under pressure from the U.S. Congress and U.S. interest groups opposed to any opening toward Iran, President Bill Clinton issued an executive order banning U.S. companies from investing in Iran's energy sector. A year later, the Iran-Libya Sanctions Act was passed, which penalizes foreign companies that invest more than $20 million in Iran's energy industry. In reaction, in 1997 Tehran signed a $2 billion deal with the French oil and gas company Total.

Meanwhile, many Western companies that have continued to want to do business in Iran have struggled to bid for its huge and untapped natural gas reserves. And to immunize itself against the effects of the sanctions and any potential boycott by the West, Iran has shifted its oil trade from the West to new markets. Before the 1979 revolution, the top five importers of Iranian oil were, in decreasing order, France, West Germany, the United Kingdom,

Italy, and Japan. By 2008, they were Japan, China, India, South Korea, and Italy. Iran has also recently helped open up the Persian Gulf to China and Russia, signing multibillion-dollar contracts with the Chinese company Sinopec and granting Russia major concessions and access to the Azadegan oil field. Khamenei has even proposed forming with Russia a natural gas cartel modeled after OPEC.

Despite U.S. opposition, Iran has also made good progress on the construction of a so-called peace pipeline that would carry gas from the Persian Gulf to India through Pakistan, a project that would strengthen Iran's position as a major source of energy for those two countries. Nor should one underestimate the negative long-term implications for U.S. interests of China's and Russia's increasing involvement in the Persian Gulf, which Iran has facilitated, or of Tehran's recent move to use the euro in its international transactions, which has weakened the dollar. On the other hand, the sanctions have hurt Iran badly. Its plan for gas and oil pipelines that would connect the Persian Gulf to the Caspian Sea has stalled because of the restrictions. And its oil industry has been deprived of access to important modern technologies: as a result, Iran's oil production today remains significantly below what it was in 1979. In other words, the sanctions have been a lose-lose economic proposition for both the United States and Iran.

RISING IN THE REGION

AFTER THREE decades of Washington's containment policies, Iran has nonetheless emerged as a regional power. The collapse of the Soviet Union allowed Tehran to expand its influence in the former Soviet republics, many of which it shares historical ties with. A decade later, the United States accelerated the process by overthrowing the Taliban and Saddam Hussein, Iran's neighboring nemeses. And by failing to reactivate the Arab-Israeli peace process and mismanaging the occupation of Iraq,

Washington created enticing opportunities for Iran to expand its power. For the first time in a long while, Iran's influence now radiates west, north, and east. Iran now rightly considers itself an indispensable regional player.

These ambitions pit Tehran against Washington. As Mohsen Rezai, a former commander of the Revolutionary Guards, stated in 2007, "It is our principal and indisputable right to become a regional power," and the United States "would like to prevent us from playing such a role." According to a March 2007 article in *The New York Times*, a recent UN sanctions package against Iran's nuclear program was passed in order to rein in what U.S. officials saw as "Tehran's ambitions to become the dominant military power in the Persian Gulf and across the broader Middle East."

A pivotal element of Iran's strategy of neutralizing the United States' containment policy is to create spheres of influence in Syria, Lebanon, and among the Palestinians, as well as in Afghanistan and Iraq, by supporting pro-Iranian organizations and networks there. (As Rezai put it, "Iran has no meaning without Iraq, Lebanon, Palestine, and Syria.") An especially controversial part of this strategy is Iran's support for Syria, Hezbollah, Palestinian Islamic Jihad, and Hamas—the rejectionist front in the Arab-Israeli conflict. Iran's three-decade-long alliance with Syria is one of the most enduring alliances between Middle Eastern Muslim countries since the end of World War II. Iran's support of the Shiites of Lebanon and the Palestinians goes back many years. Rafsanjani was incarcerated in the 1960s for translating a pro-Palestinian book into Persian; Khomeini condemned the shah in 1964 for his de facto recognition of Israel; Khomeini also authorized Hassan Nasrallah, the leader of Hezbollah, to collect religious taxes on his behalf in support of the Lebanese Shiites; and many of Iran's current leaders received training in Lebanon in the 1960s and 1970s. At first, Iran's support for Hezbollah and the Palestinians had an ideological basis; now, it has a strategic rationale. It gives Tehran strategic depth in the heart of the Sunni Arab world and in Israel's backyard, which translates into a retaliatory capacity against Israel, as well as bargaining power in any future negotiations with the United States. Moreover, after centuries of using its influence mostly to defend Shiites, Iran is now increasingly trying to transcend the sectarian divide by supporting the Sunni groups Hamas and Palestinian Islamic Jihad. This, in turn, has undermined the regional position of such powerful Sunni countries as Egypt and Saudi Arabia.

That said, Iran's financial and logistical support for Hamas and Islamic Jihad should not be exaggerated. Tehran remains a peripheral player in the Arab-Israeli conflict. It has no compelling national interest in the dispute and is simply taking advantage of the failure of the peace process between Israel and the Palestinians. What makes Iran an influential player is not its financial support alone—Saudi Arabia and other Arab countries contribute substantially more to the Palestinians—but also the model of resistance it champions. Iran has helped Hezbollah develop an approach that combines Islamic solidarity, populism, some trappings of democracy, strict organizational discipline, extensive economic and social support for the needy masses, and pervasive anticolonial and anti-Western sentiments—all in an effort to mobilize the streets of the Islamic world against Israel and the United States and expand its own power. The effectiveness of that model, and of its asymmetric strategies, was on display during Hezbollah's 34-day war with Israel in 2006. The group's use of antitank missiles and portable rockets, which Israel claimed Iran had provided—a charge Iran has denied—inflicted enough damage on Israeli cities to create havoc and mass fear. Hezbollah appeared to have won because Israel could not score a decisive victory against it; the conflict marked the first time that an Arab force was not humiliatingly defeated by Israel. It boosted Hezbollah's popularity in many Sunni countries, gave Iran more credibility in the region, and undermined Washington's traditional allies, such as Egypt and Saudi Arabia, which had not supported Hezbollah. The war, along with the chaos in Afghanistan and Iraq and what the Iran expert Vali Nasr has called "the Shiite revival," has convinced Tehran that a new order is emerging in the Middle East: the United States no longer dominates, and Iran now plays a major role.

WHERE THE HARD THINGS ARE

THE COMPLICATED nature of the U.S.-Iranian relationship is most evident in Afghanistan and Iraq, where the convergences and divergences of the two sides' interests are the clearest. After the Soviet occupation of Afghanistan in 1979, Tehran became intensely engaged with its neighbor, and Iran subsequently became home to some two million Afghan refugees. Gradually, throughout the 1980s, it built new alliances and new networks with Shiite and Persian- and Dari-speaking minorities. (As the Afghanistan expert Barnett Rubin has put it, during that period, "ironically, the United States was indirectly aligned with 'fundamentalists' while Iran courted the 'moderates.'") Then, in the 1990s, while Pakistan and Saudi Arabia were providing critical support to the Taliban government, which itself backed al Qaeda, Tehran created a sphere of resistance in Afghanistan by supporting the Northern Alliance— a force that cooperated with the invading U.S. troops in 2001 in order to liberate Afghanistan from the Taliban. In helping dismantle the Taliban, in other words, Tehran effectively sided with the U.S. government—even providing Washington with intelligence.

Tehran maintained its policy toward Afghanistan even after U.S. President George W. Bush said Iran belonged to "an axis of evil." Today, still, it entertains close relations with the pro-U.S. government of Afghan President Hamid Karzai. And the convergence between Tehran's interests and Washington's interests in Afghanistan remains substantial. Both want to keep the country stable and prevent the Taliban's resurgence. Both want to control and possibly eliminate drug trafficking, the economic backbone of the region's terrorists and warlords. Both want to defeat al Qaeda (which considers Shiism to be a heresy). And both want to eventually rebuild Afghanistan.

At the same time, Iran's heavy involvement in the reconstruction of Afghanistan has allowed it to create a sphere of economic influence in the region around Herat, one of the most prosperous regions in the country. This, in turn, has helped stabilize the area by preventing al Qaeda and the Taliban from infiltrating it. Iran has also empowered the historically marginalized Afghan Shiites, such as the Hazara and the Qizilbash, who constitute about 20 percent of the Afghan population. At a donors' conference in Tokyo in January 2002, Iran pledged $560 million for Afghanistan's reconstruction, or approximately 12 percent of the total $4.5 billion in international reconstruction assistance that was promised then. During a donors' conference in London in 2006, it pledged an additional $100 million. And unlike many other donors, it has delivered most of its promised assistance. The bulk of the funds are targeted at developing projects for infrastructure, education, agriculture, power generation, and telecommunications. Iran hopes to become a hub for the transit of goods and services between the Persian Gulf and Afghanistan, Central Asia, and possibly also China.

This quest for influence in Afghanistan pits Iran against the United States in some ways. For example, Tehran opposes the establishment of permanent U.S. bases in Afghanistan. And to ensure that Washington will not be able to use Afghanistan as a launching point for an attack on Iran, Tehran is pressuring Kabul to distance itself from Washington. Uncertain about Afghanistan's future and Washington's intentions in the country, Iran is keeping its options open and trying to increase all its possible retaliatory capabilities against the United States. It maintains close ties with the Northern Alliance, as well as with warlords such as Ismail Khan, various Shiite organizations, and the insurgent leader Gulbuddin Hekmatyar and other anti-American fighters. It is turning the region around Herat into a sphere of influence: the bazaars there are loaded with Iranian goods, the area receives the bulk of Iran's investments in the country, and the Revolutionary Guards are reportedly visible and active.

The United States and Iran have tried to strike a fine balance in Iraq as well, but with much less success. If anything, Iraq has become center stage for their rivalry; there they have some common goals but also many more diverging ones. Iran's top strategic priority in Iraq is to establish a friendly, preferably Shiite government that is sufficiently powerful to impose order in the country but not powerful enough to pose a serious security threat to Iran, as Saddam did. Iran was the first country in the region to recognize the post-Saddam government in Baghdad. Since then, it has provided Baghdad with more support than even the staunchest of the United States' allies. It has a close relationship with the two parties that dominate the government of Prime Minister Nouri al-Maliki, as well as with the two major Kurdish parties. Like Washington, Tehran supports Iraq's stability, its new constitution, and its electoral democracy, albeit in the parochial interest of ensuring the dominance of the country's Shiite majority. Like Washington, Tehran opposes Iraq's Balkanization, in its case partly for fear that such fragmentation could incite secessionist movements within Iran's own ethnically rich population. And like Washington, Iran considers al Qaeda in Iraq to be an enemy and seeks to eliminate it.

But as in Afghanistan, Iran is eager to engage in Iraq's reconstruction mainly in order to create an economic sphere of influence in the country, especially in the predominantly Shiite south, where many people of Persian descent live. It has pledged to spend more than $1 billion for Iraq's reconstruction. Tehran seems to believe that with its existing influence in southern Iraq, including close ties to the major Shiite seminaries in Najaf, it can transform the region into a kind of southern Lebanon, creating a ministate within a state.

And then there are some major disagreements between Tehran and Washington. Tehran is determined to keep Washington mired in Iraq and prevent it from scoring a clear victory there. During the sectarian violence in 2004–7, Tehran supplied weapons to Shiite insurgents in Iraq, who then used them against U.S.

troops. It supported the Mahdi Army and its founder, Muqtada al-Sadr, the radical Shiite cleric who opposes the U.S. presence in Iraq. Tehran is also vehemently opposed to the establishment of permanent U.S. bases in Iraq, for fear, as with those in Afghanistan, that the United States could use them to attack Iran. The status-of-forces agreement signed by the United States and Iraq in 2008 does seem to have diminished some of Iran's concerns, however. The agreement stipulates that U.S. forces will withdraw from Iraq no later than December 31, 2011, and that "Iraqi land, sea, and air shall not be used as a launching or transit point for attacks against other countries."

Iran's policies toward Iraq in the past few years suggest that when Iran feels threatened and its legitimate security needs and national interests are ignored or undermined, it tends to act more mischievously than when it feels secure. Its Iraq policy, therefore, is directly correlated with its perception of the threat posed by the United States. The security talks between Tehran and Washington launched at the urging of the Iraqi government in 2005 are thus very important. After these meetings began, and after the U.S. government launched its "surge" strategy in Iraq, the level of violence in Iraq subsided. Iran played a role in stabilizing the situation by pressuring its allies, including the Mahdi Army, to refrain from violence against Sunnis or U.S. troops. The simple fact that Baghdad is a close ally of both Tehran and Washington offers a chance for those two governments to build on their interests in Iraq.

FULL ENGAGEMENT

ANTI-AMERICANISM IS not an insurmountable obstacle to normalizing relations with Iran. For one thing, Iran's elites are heterogeneous; they consist of two rival factions, both of which have come to favor, like a significant portion of the population, normalizing relations with the United States. For another, *maslehat*, or "expediency," is a defining feature of Iranian politics. Even the most ideological of Iran's leaders favor a cost-benefit approach to decision-making. According to the 2007 U.S. National Intelligence Estimate, Iran halted its nuclear weapons program in 2003 based on a cost-benefit calculation. Although the accuracy of that conclusion is debated, there is no question that Tehran has often resorted to that approach. When Iran needed advanced weapons during the Iran-Iraq War, Khomeini approved secret dealings with Israel and the United States, culminating in the Iran-contra fiasco. Despite its general opposition to the presence of U.S. troops in the region, Tehran remained actively neutral during the 1991 Persian Gulf War, seeing it as an opportunity to weaken its archenemy Saddam and improve relations with the West. The Revolutionary Guards, the most ideological group in the Iranian armed forces, rubbed shoulders with U.S. forces when they assisted the Northern Alliance in overthrowing the Taliban in 2001. Far from being a suicidally ideological regime, Tehran seeks to ensure the survival of the Islamic Republic while advancing the country's interests through negotiations.

Iranian policy toward the United States has a logic. It is a logic driven not by a single faction or a single issue but by a stable and institutionalized system of governance with both authoritarian and democratic features, with domestic constituencies and long-standing international alliances. It is a logic that made Iran into a regional power with substantial influence in Afghanistan, Iraq, Lebanon, and the Palestinian territories, and among millions of Muslims around the world. And it is a logic that, despite mounting international pressure, has made it possible for Iran to make advances in asymmetric warfare, nuclear technology, uranium enrichment, and missile and satellite technologies. Now, Iran legitimately demands that Washington recognize these advances and Tehran's new role as a major regional power.

Unless Washington understands that Tehran's U.S. policy has a rationale, it will not be able to develop a reasonable long-term strategy toward Iran. Invading the country is not a viable option. Nor are so-called surgical strikes against Iran's nuclear facilities, which would most likely lead to a protracted retaliation by Iran; a Tehran more defiant and more determined to become a nuclear weapons power; more terrorism; greater instability in Afghanistan, Iraq, Lebanon, and the Persian Gulf; and higher oil prices.

The challenge for the U.S. government is to give Iran incentives to reevaluate its strategy toward the United States. A carrot-and-stick approach designed to stop progress on Iran's nuclear program is unlikely to work. Focusing on a few contentious issues, such as Iran's uranium-enrichment activities, would do little to change the fundamental logic of Iran's U.S. policy. Moreover, the stick part of that approach would only strengthen the anti-American constituencies in Iran while hurting its people. Nor will democracy promotion work. More a feel-good fantasy than a viable strategy, this approach misleadingly assumes that democracy can be exported, like cars, or imposed by force and that a democratic Iran would no longer have any serious conflicts with the United States or pursue nuclear ambitions. Iran was considerably more democratic under Mosaddeq than under the shah, and yet its relations with the United States were much worse then.

A better approach is a strategy of full engagement, one predicated on gradually increasing economic, educational, and cultural exchanges between the two countries; exploiting the commonalities shared by their governments; and establishing concrete institutional mechanisms to manage their remaining differences. Washington must recognize that there is no diplomatic magic wand that can fix its "Iran problem" overnight; normalizing U.S.-Iranian relations will be a long and difficult process. Unless Tehran and Washington make a strategic decision to normalize relations, the many forces that continue to pull them apart are likely to derail the process.

As a first step, the United States should allay Iran's fears about regime change. It can do this by explicitly recognizing that Khamenei is the center of gravity in Iran's decision-making process and establishing a line of communication with his office. Holding direct, comprehensive, and unconditional negotiations with the Iranian government is Washington's least bad option.

The two countries' negotiating teams must meet face-to-face to learn firsthand about each other's priorities and interests on all the important issues and break the psychological barriers that have kept the parties apart for three decades. Meanwhile, Washington should provide assurances to Israel and its Arab allies that they should not fear its rapprochement with Tehran and that Iran's nuclear policy will remain the main item on the United States' Iran agenda.

As the Obama administration reviews its options when it comes to Iran, it would do well to examine how, three decades ago, President Richard Nixon brought China back into the community of nations. It took almost eight years after the secret trip by Henry Kissinger, then U.S. national security adviser, to Beijing in 1971 for the United States and China to establish diplomatic relations. Anti-Americanism under Mao Zedong, China's support for North Vietnam, and China's arsenal of nuclear weapons were infinitely more threatening to the United States then than Iran's policies are now. Yet Nixon and Kissinger had the foresight to map out a new strategic landscape for Beijing. They did not punish it for its policies of the past; they gave it a reason to want something better in the future. And then the two countries built a better relationship on their common recognition of the threat posed by Soviet expansionism. Washington can, and should, do something similar with Tehran today and finally end three decades of hostility by highlighting the two governments' shared interests in defeating al Qaeda and stabilizing Afghanistan and Iraq. Tehran, for its part, must recognize that without some kind of understanding with Washington over the issues that matter to the U.S. government, it will not be able to fully benefit from its recent ascent as a regional power—and could even lose much of what it has gained.❷

Debating the Options

Regime Change and Its Limits

Richard N. Haass

Foreign Affairs, July/August 2005

ARMED AND DANGEROUS

ALTHOUGH A third of the "axis of evil" is now occupied by U.S. forces, the other two thirds—North Korea and Iran—remain clear threats to U.S. interests. Consider North Korea: in February 2005, Pyongyang announced that it had nuclear weapons, and it is now thought to have several of them, or at least the material to build them. Over time, if the United States does nothing, North Korea's arsenal will surely grow, as will the amount of its fissile material. The results of this growth will be destabilizing and potentially disastrous: a sizable North Korean nuclear arsenal might well stimulate similar weapons programs in both Japan and South Korea, diminishing the region's stability. The repercussions could also spread far beyond Northeast Asia if Pyongyang decides to sell its new weapons or nuclear fuel for hard currency—as it has with drugs and missile technology in the past.

Iran, for its part, also has a nuclear weapons program, which may not be as advanced as North Korea's but is much further

---

RICHARD N. HAASS is President of the Council on Foreign Relations. He was Director of the State Department's Policy Planning Staff from 2001 to 2003. This article is drawn from his recently published book, *The Opportunity: America's Moment to Alter History's Course.*

along than almost anyone realized only a few years ago. Building on efforts that began under the shah, Iran has assembled many of the elements needed for a uranium-enrichment program with military potential. Magnifying Washington's concern, Iran has a history of concealing its nuclear program, as well as supporting terrorism and developing medium-range missiles.

Thus far, the Bush administration has consistently shown that it would rather resolve all of these challenges through regime change in Tehran and Pyongyang. It is not hard to fathom why: regime change is less distasteful than diplomacy and less dangerous than living with new nuclear states. There is only one problem: it is highly unlikely to have the desired effect soon enough.

REVOLUTION AND EVOLUTION

REGIME CHANGE allows a state to solve its problems with another state by removing the offensive regime there and replacing it with a less offensive one. In the case of North Korea or Iran, this would mean installing a regime that either would not pursue nuclear weapons or, if it did, would be so different in character that the prospect would be much less worrisome.

Using regime change as a policy panacea is nothing new. Nor are the challenges posed by repressive countries possessing threatening weaponry; these are certainly not exclusively post–Cold War or post–September 11 phenomena. Indeed, the Cold War itself can be understood as a prolonged confrontation with a state of precisely this sort; the Soviet Union threatened the United States by what it did beyond its borders and offended Americans by what it did within them. So had Nazi Germany and imperial Japan before it.

The Roosevelt administration ultimately chose to deal with Germany and Japan through a policy of regime change, seeking not simply to defeat them on the battlefield and reverse their conquests but to continue war until the regimes in Berlin and Tokyo were ousted and something much better was firmly ensconced.

It took years of armed occupation and intrusive involvement in the internal politics of both countries—what is known today as nation building—to achieve that latter objective.

The U.S. approach to the Soviet Union, however, was markedly different. After World War II, when Moscow emerged as Washington's principal global rival and threat, "rollback" became something of a popular concept. Yet the potential for a nuclear war in which there would be no winners regardless of who struck first tempered U.S. policy. Seeking regime change, or rollback, was deemed too risky, even reckless, given what could result if a desperate Soviet leadership lashed out with all the force at its disposal.

Simply acquiescing to Soviet behavior at home and abroad, however, was not acceptable to Washington either. The result was a policy of "containment," which George Kennan (then a U.S. diplomat in Moscow) helped formulate in his "long telegram," which ultimately found its way into this magazine in 1947. Containment was never as modest a policy as its critics alleged. Although it prescribed resisting Moscow's attempts to spread communism and expand Soviet influence, it also had a second, less cited dimension.

"It is entirely possible," Kennan wrote,

> for the United States to influence by its actions the internal developments, both within Russia and throughout the international Communist movement.... The United States has it in its power to increase enormously the strains under which Soviet policy must operate, to force upon the Kremlin a far greater degree of moderation and circumspection than [the Kremlin] has had to observe in recent years, and in this way to promote tendencies which must eventually find their outlet in either the break-up or the gradual mellowing of Soviet power.

In other words, containment's second, subordinate goal was regime change. It eventually achieved this end through incremental means. But this method was so gradual (it took more than 40 years to succeed) that it could better be understood as regime evolution, and it took a back seat to containing Soviet advances. Whereas regime change (as the Bush administration uses the term) tends to be direct and immediate and to involve the use of military force or covert action, as well as attempts to isolate both politically and economically the government in question, regime evolution tends to be indirect and gradual and to involve the use of foreign policy tools other than military force.

Advocates of regime change generally reject most, sometimes any, dealings with the regime in question, lest the process of interaction or engagement somehow buttress the offending government. Diplomacy is therefore marginalized, as it has been in U.S. Cuba policy for 40 years, and as it has been more recently in U.S. policy toward both North Korea and Iran.

Regime evolution, however, accepts the need for give-and-take. The United States carried out an active diplomacy with the Soviet Union throughout the Cold War. It mattered not whether the policy was characterized as "peaceful coexistence" or, somewhat more optimistically, as "détente"; either way, the United States was prepared to deal with the Soviet Union when doing so served U.S. interests. Containment took precedence over rollback, or regime change, and influencing Soviet foreign policy took precedence over influencing Soviet behavior at home. This did not mean the United States ignored questions of what was going on inside the Soviet Union—it did not, as evidenced by sustained U.S. support for radio broadcasts addressed to the Soviet people, for individual human rights cases, and for the right to emigrate. But Washington did not accord these issues the same weight as Soviet foreign policy.

To understand how this process worked, consider arms control, one realm of intense U.S.-Soviet involvement. U.S. officials regularly negotiated with their Soviet counterparts and entered into agreements to limit weapons, particularly nuclear ones. Such a policy may have prolonged the Soviet regime, since it accorded Moscow a unique and prominent international standing and placed curbs on a costly arms race that might have hastened the regime's demise (given the country's weak economic base). Still, successive U.S. administrations prudently deemed avoiding war and regulating U.S.-Soviet arms competition higher goals.

A similar rationale motivated the United States' economic dealings with the Soviet Union. Concern that bilateral trade could buttress the Soviet government was overridden by the view that trade deals would also give the Soviets a stake in better relations with the United States and the West and thereby rein in any Soviet temptation to challenge violently the status quo.

In the end, the Soviet regime did change. Historians will continue to debate how much of this was due to internal flaws in the Soviet system and how much resulted from U.S. and Western policy. The easy answer is that both forces were effective. The important thing is that an end did come, and it came peacefully. The third great conflict of the twentieth century, like the first two, ended with the result desired by the United States. Unlike the outcomes of the first two conflicts, however, this one was achieved without total war.

EASIER SAID THAN DONE

THE SOVIET experience holds important lessons for current U.S. foreign policy. Removing odious leaders—"regime ouster"— is no easy thing. The Soviet Union survived for nearly three-quarters of a century. The United States found it difficult to locate and arrest Manuel Noriega in Panama in 1989 and impossible to oust Mohamed Farah Aideed in Somalia in 1993. Fidel Castro remains ensconced in Havana today.

Regime replacement, the second step in regime change, is even more difficult, however. In the end, toppling Saddam Hussein was easy compared with putting in place a new Iraqi government that could run a secure, viable country. Although the Iraq venture was made far more expensive and difficult than necessary by Washington's poor planning and questionable decisions, it is possible it would not have gone more smoothly even had Iraq's occupation been approached differently. And occupations elsewhere will not be much easier. The rise of nationalism, together with globalization (and the increased availability of powerful means of resistance), may have doomed prolonged occupations of foreign countries by sharply increasing their human, military, and economic costs.

Indeed, the uncertainties surrounding regime change make it an unreliable approach for dealing with specific problems such as a nuclear weapons program in an unfriendly state. Neither North Korea nor Iran appears to be on the brink of dramatic domestic change. A decade ago, many believed that North Korea was near collapse, yet the regime still stands, and it may persist for years more, notwithstanding North Korea's impoverishment, its cruel and eccentric leadership, and its utter lack of freedom. Iran, too, is unlikely to throw off its current clerical leaders, despite their unpopularity. Even if these assessments ultimately prove incorrect, regime change cannot be counted on to come quickly enough to remove the nuclear threats now posed by these countries.

Unless, that is, the United States is prepared to invade them. But the expense of this approach would be enormous. Pyongyang's conventional military power could inflict great loss of life and physical destruction on South Korea, and its nuclear weapons could obviously increase such costs dramatically. Many U.S. military personnel (including some of the more than 30,000 currently stationed in South Korea, along with reinforcements who would be sent) would lose their lives. The United States could and would win such a war, but only at great cost to itself, the region, and the rest of the world. The same goes for war with Iran. That country is roughly the size of Alaska and has 70 million people, roughly three times as many as Iraq—more than enough to make any occupation costly, miserable, and futile for the United States.

Using more indirect tools to bring about regime evolution, instead of change, might well work but would take years, if not decades. Achieving regime evolution requires the strategic use of television, radio, and the Internet. Admission to the World Trade Organization (WTO) could be offered in return for fundamental economic reforms, ones that are, by their nature, also political. Rhetorical support for change can also help, as can direct assistance to nongovernmental organizations and other elements of civil society. Economic and political incentives should be made available to the target country if it is willing to adopt policies that reduce threats and that create more freedom and space for independent economic and political activity; in the absence of such changes, targeted sanctions should be considered. Trade and personnel exchanges can open a closed society to new ideas. Over the past few decades, there have been dozens of cases of successful regime evolution in the former Soviet bloc, Latin America, and Asia, and there is no reason such patterns could not be repeated elsewhere if the United States makes the investment and takes the necessary time. Odious or dangerous regimes should never be neglected, but the safest and best way to encourage their moderation or implosion is to smother them with policies that force them to open up to and deal with the outside world.

MILITARY MEANS

ONE OTHER alternative for dealing with Pyongyang's and Tehran's nuclear programs is the limited use of military force. Such attacks could take two forms. One is a preemptive strike, akin to what Israel did in 1967 when, learning of an imminent Egyptian attack, it hit the Egyptians first. For such an attack to work, however, the intelligence assessment of the threat must be near 100 percent accurate, confirming that the danger is in fact imminent and that there are no other available means to stop it. Under such rare circumstances, it is widely viewed that a state enjoys the right to strike before it is certain to be struck. This is preemption in the classical sense—something quite different from President George W. Bush's use of the term, which in fact is better understood as prevention.

The problem for U.S. policymakers today is that neither situation—neither that with North Korea nor that with Iran—is likely to satisfy the conditions that warrant a preemptive strike in the traditional sense. Instead, available intelligence will probably be questionable, the threats uncertain and in no way clearly imminent, and the military option but one of several policies available. Under such circumstances, any U.S. attack would be preventive, not preemptive—the use of force against a gathering but not imminent threat.

There are some precedents for preventive strikes, such as Israel's attack on Iraq's Osirak nuclear complex in 1981 or the U.S.-led invasion of Iraq some two decades later. But preventive attacks always pose serious problems. For one thing, it is all but impossible to get international support for them. For another, they are quite difficult to carry out successfully; indeed, given the secrecy surrounding nuclear programs, the level of intelligence needed to effectively cripple them through a military attack can be impossible to attain.

It is this last consideration—of feasibility—that is likely to determine the use of preventive strikes in the future. It is not just a question of what constitutes North Korea's nuclear weapons program or where it is. Washington could in principle strike other targets valued by Pyongyang to coerce it into meeting U.S. and international demands regarding its nuclear programs. It is not clear, however, whether Washington could get political support for such attacks or that they would have the desired effect. In fact, South Korea, Japan, China, and Russia are likely to oppose any action that could lead to a war on the Korean Peninsula that would kill hundreds of thousands and destroy the economy of South Korea and of the region more generally.

Using preventive strikes to destroy Iran's developing weapons program would also be much easier said than done, given the imperfect nature of the intelligence on Iran's program and the operational challenges of attacking its dispersed and buried nuclear facilities. U.S. strikes might succeed in destroying part of Iran's weapons program and set it back by months or even years. But even if this were to occur, Iran would surely reconstitute its program in a manner that would make future strikes even more difficult. Moreover, Iran has the ability to retaliate by unleashing terrorism (using Hamas and Hezbollah) against Israel and the United States or by promoting instability in Iraq, Afghanistan, and Saudi Arabia. A U.S. strike on Iran would also further anger the Arab and Muslim worlds, where many already resent the double standard of U.S. and international acceptance of Israel's and India's nuclear weapons programs. Much of the Iranian population, currently alienated from the regime, would likely rally around it in the case of a foreign attack, making external efforts to bring about regime change that much more unlikely to succeed. Attacking Iran would also lead to sharp and possibly prolonged increases in the price of oil, which could trigger a global economic crisis. Nor would the United States avoid these costs if Israel carried out the strike (a scenario suggested by Vice President Dick Cheney in January 2005), since Israel would be widely viewed as doing the United States' bidding.

TALK FIRST

ANOTHER ALTERNATIVE policy for meeting the nuclear challenge posed by Iran and North Korea would be to emphasize diplomacy. North Korea and Iran could be promised a number of benefits, including economic assistance, security assurances, and greater political standing, if they satisfied U.S. and international concerns regarding their nuclear programs. They could also be presented with clear penalties in case they fail to cooperate adequately. Such penalties could include diplomatic and economic sanctions and, in the most dire circumstances, military attack.

It is far from clear, however, whether any such agreement could actually be negotiated. North Korea may well decide that possessing nuclear weapons is the best way to deter a U.S.-led military intervention and to earn hard currency—and thus refuse to give up such weapons. Iran, too, may decide that nuclear weapons are too useful as a deterrent and a means to acquire regional influence.

Even if these states agreed to give up their weapons, moreover, there is no guarantee that they would honor their agreements. North Korea has already breached a 1992 accord with South Korea to keep the peninsula free of nuclear weapons and violated the spirit (if not necessarily the letter) of the 1994 U.S.–North Korean Agreed Framework. Iran, for its part, has failed to fulfill its obligations to notify the International Atomic Energy Agency (IAEA) of its uranium-enrichment activities, as it is required to under a safeguards agreement Tehran signed pursuant to the Nonproliferation Treaty.

Given their records, North Korea and Iran could be expected to exploit the time any negotiation would buy them to enhance their nuclear capabilities. Even absent such bad faith, essentially rewarding a country such as North Korea with alternative energy sources and various political and economic benefits for its having once invested in nuclear weapons could have the perverse effect of encouraging proliferation elsewhere. It might give other countries an incentive to follow suit in the belief that they, too, will eventually be rewarded for their bad behavior.

Despite these problems, however, diplomacy remains an attractive option, both because it could succeed and because only by first making a good-faith effort will the United States have a chance of getting the necessary regional and international backing for then pursuing a more confrontational tack.

In fact, the United States (working with China, Japan, Russia, and South Korea) has already initiated a series of discussions with North Korea in order to convince it to abandon its nuclear weapons program. Pyongyang, however, rejected the incentives Washington offered it last year, and the failure to include any clear penalties in the deal put little pressure on North Korea to compromise. Neither the carrot nor the stick was adequate. In addition, the Bush administration lost valuable time by resisting the prospect of bilateral talks with North Korea. This was a mistake; it matters little whether China, Japan, South Korea, and Russia are physically in the room so long as the United States coordinates its policies with them.

The best path available now is to continue to work with these states on a diplomatic package that would give North Korea security assurances, energy assistance, and specified political and economic benefits in exchange for forgoing its nuclear programs (fuel and weapons alike) and agreeing to robust international inspections. Sequence matters in all this; it is unrealistic to expect North Korea to satisfy all nuclear-related requirements before it receives any benefits. Washington and its partners should also agree on what economic and political sanctions would be imposed on Pyongyang if it failed to accept such an agreement by a specified date or if it crossed a red line, such as by testing a nuclear device.

China's role is central to any such diplomatic undertaking. Although Beijing's influence on North Korea is limited, it is greater than any other country's. China is the source of much of North Korea's energy and is its principal trading partner. But Beijing, while willing to apply some pressure, seems reluctant to insist, possibly out of fear that if Kim Jong Il's regime begins to collapse, war will break out and refugees will flood China. As a result, China has seemed more interested in placing a lid on the North Korea problem than in actually resolving it.

Washington must try to persuade Beijing to use all of its influence to convince Pyongyang to abandon its nuclear weapons program. To this end, China's leaders should understand that the North Korea problem is a test case of China's willingness to become a true strategic partner of the United States. It would also help if the U.S. government were to reassure China's leaders about its long-term thinking on Northeast Asia, namely, that the United States is firmly opposed to the emergence of any new nuclear weapons state in the region, be it Japan, a unified Korea, or Taiwan.

Addressing Iran's nuclear program will require an international proposal offering Tehran the nuclear fuel it says it requires for power generation, but not direct access to or control of the fuel itself. Such an offer could be made to Iran alone. But to improve its attractiveness, the deal should be put forward as a new global policy, in which no entity other than the five acknowledged nuclear weapons states and the IAEA would be permitted to control nuclear fuel. To secure Iran's agreement, the country, which is currently subject to numerous U.S. economic sanctions, could be offered various economic inducements and security assurances akin to those being considered for North Korea. In exchange for these benefits, Iran (again like North Korea) would be expected to convince the world, by allowing intrusive inspections, that it is not developing nuclear weapons or producing the fissile material they require. U.S. policy currently seems to be headed in this direction, but Washington needs to offer more than simply ending its blockage of Iran's admission to the WTO or its purchase of spare parts for aircraft. For their part, Europe and Russia, as well as China, must commit to meaningful sanctions in the event Iran violates the agreement. This is a moment for creative specificity, not ambiguity.

Even if such tactics are used, it remains possible (some would say likely) that diplomacy with Iran will fail, either because of insufficient international support or because many in Iran want to proceed with uranium enrichment or develop nuclear weapons regardless of the cost. As with North Korea, however, the diplomatic option is nonetheless worth pursuing, given the costs of every other approach and given that the only chance for building international support for (or even acceptance of) a more aggressive strategy is to first make a good-faith effort to resolve matters diplomatically.

LIVING WITH PROLIFERATION

THERE IS always the option of accepting a de facto nuclear status for North Korea and Iran. This is the default option if regime change yields no dramatic result, the military option is rejected, and diplomacy fails. And it would be similar to what has already become the U.S. and international approach to Israel, India, and Pakistan. There would have to be, however, one big difference: given the bellicose history and nature of both North

Korea and Iran, the United States would need to introduce an extra element of deterrence to discourage either government from using a nuclear weapon or transferring critical technologies, fuel, or weapons to other states or to terrorist groups. To this end, the United States should declare publicly that any government that uses weapons of mass destruction, threatens to use them, or knowingly transfers WMD or key materials to third parties opens itself up to the strongest reprisals, including attack and removal from power. This message should be accompanied by a concerted diplomatic effort to get the other major powers to sign on to such a policy. Such moves would add teeth to Security Council resolutions and international conventions that already forbid states from facilitating nuclear terrorism in any way.

Even with such international statements, this approach would be inherently risky: accepting a North Korean nuclear arsenal might mean accepting the perpetuation of a desperate, failing government that could well try secretly to transfer nuclear material to terrorists in exchange for much-needed money. Accepting the existence of a nuclear-armed Iran implies a similar bargain. And in both cases, deterrence might not work.

What is more, even if deterrence did work, accepting and learning to live with a nuclear-armed North Korea or Iran would not be cost free. As suggested above, if North Korea is allowed to retain nuclear weapons, this could prompt Japan, South Korea, or other states to seek to acquire them as well. Keeping the peace in a nuclear Northeast Asia would be no easy feat given the historical animosities, the latent rivalries, and the lack of institutional mechanisms for promoting regional confidence and stability.

The same goes for the Middle East. A nuclear Iran could well cause Egypt, Saudi Arabia, Syria, and even Iraq to consider developing a similar capability, although it might take them longer to catch up due to their lack of an advanced industrial base. And keeping the peace between a half dozen nuclear-armed states that are suspicious of, if not downright hostile toward, one another would be extremely difficult. The emergence of new nuclear weapons states would also dramatically increase the risk that these weapons or their components would fall into the hands of terrorists, whether by accident or design.

ALL TOGETHER NOW

REGIME CHANGE, limited military action, diplomacy, and deterrence can all be considered as alternative policies. They are better understood, however, as components of a single comprehensive approach toward states such as North Korea and Iran. Deterrence is a way to make the best of a bad situation. Military action or, more precisely, the threat of it can buttress diplomatic prospects. But diplomacy should be the heart of U.S. policy toward both countries—because it could succeed, because it must be shown to have failed before there is any chance of garnering support for other policies, and because all the other options are so unattractive.

As for regime change, it is best viewed as a complement to diplomacy and deterrence. It is essential to appreciate not only the limits of regime change but also its nature. A refusal to engage tyrannies allows them to wrap themselves in nationalism and to maintain control; offering regimes enhanced security and economic and political interaction if they meet specified requirements can deny them their rationale for tight control and their ability to maintain it. A foreign policy that chooses to integrate, not isolate, despotic regimes can be the Trojan horse that moderates their behavior in the short run and their nature in the long run. It is time Washington put this thinking to the test, toward what remains of the axis of evil. Delay is no longer an option, and drift is not a strategy.◉

How to Keep the Bomb From Iran

Scott D. Sagan

Foreign Affairs, September/October 2006

PREVENTING THE UNTHINKABLE

THE ONGOING crisis with Tehran is not the first time Washington has had to face a hostile government attempting to develop nuclear weapons. Nor is it likely to be the last. Yet the reasoning of U.S. officials now struggling to deal with Iran's nuclear ambitions is clouded by a kind of historical amnesia, which leads to both creeping fatalism about the United States' ability to keep Iran from getting the bomb and excessive optimism about the United States' ability to contain Iran if it does become a nuclear power. Proliferation fatalism and deterrence optimism reinforce each other in a disturbing way. As nuclear proliferation comes to be seen as inevitable, wishful thinking can make its consequences seem less severe, and if faith in deterrence grows, incentives to combat proliferation diminish.

A U.S. official in the executive branch anonymously told *The New York Times* in March 2006, "The reality is that most of us think the Iranians are probably going to get a weapon, or the technology to make one, sooner or later." Such proliferation fatalists argue that over the long term, it may be impossible to stop Iran—or other

---

SCOTT D. SAGAN is Professor of Political Science and Director of the Center for International Security and Cooperation at Stanford University.

states for that matter—from getting the bomb. Given the spread of nuclear technology and know-how, and the right of parties to the Nuclear Nonproliferation Treaty (NPT) to enrich uranium and separate plutonium, the argument goes, any foreign government determined to acquire nuclear weapons will eventually do so. Moreover, the 1981 Israeli attack on the Osirak nuclear reactor in Iraq may have delayed Iraq's progress, but similar air strikes are unlikely to disable Iran's capacities, since its uranium-enrichment facilities can be hidden underground or widely dispersed. Imposing economic sanctions through the UN Security Council is clearly a preferable option. But as Washington learned with India and Pakistan in the 1980s and 1990s, sanctions only increase the costs of going nuclear; they do not reduce the ability of a determined government to get the bomb.

Faced with only unattractive options to stem proliferation, some Bush administration officials are reluctantly preparing to live with a nuclear Iran. Military planners and intelligence officers have reportedly been tasked with developing strategies to deter Tehran if negotiations fail. Washington officials cry that the sky is falling whenever they face the prospect of a hostile state's getting the bomb, yet they seem to find solace in the recollection that deterrence and containment did work to maintain the peace during the Cold War. So why worry that the latest crop of rogue regimes might prove less deterrable than the Soviet Union and China? The Bush administration already appears to have adopted this logic with respect to North Korea. According to *The New York Times*, administration officials privately predict that deterrence will work against Pyongyang: "The North Koreans. . . know that a missile attack on the United States would result in the vaporization of Pyongyang," the paper quoted an official as saying. And if deterrence can work with Kim Jong Il, why not with Ayatollah Ali Khamenei? "Iran is just one instance of the [proliferation] problem, and in Iran's case, containment might work," argues Brent Scowcroft, who was national security adviser to President George H. W. Bush.

But both deterrence optimism and proliferation fatalism are wrong-headed. Deterrence optimism is based on mistaken nostalgia and a faulty analogy. Although deterrence did work with the Soviet Union and China, there were many close calls; maintaining nuclear peace during the Cold War was far more difficult and uncertain than U.S. officials and the American public seem to remember today. Furthermore, a nuclear Iran would look a lot less like the totalitarian Soviet Union and the People's Republic of China and a lot more like Pakistan, Iran's unstable neighbor—a far more frightening prospect. Fatalism about nuclear proliferation is equally unwarranted. Although the United States did fail to prevent its major Cold War rivals from developing nuclear arsenals, many other countries curbed their own nuclear ambitions. After flirting with nuclear programs in the 1960s, West Germany and Japan decided that following the NPT and relying on the protection of the U.S. nuclear umbrella would bring them greater security in the future; South Korea and Taiwan gave up covert nuclear programs when the United States threatened to sever security relations with them; North Korea froze its plutonium production in the 1990s; and Libya dismantled its nascent nuclear program in 2003.

Given these facts, Washington should work harder to prevent the unthinkable rather than accept what falsely appears to be inevitable. The lesson to be drawn from the history of nonproliferation is not that all states eyeing the bomb eventually get it but that nonproliferation efforts succeed when the United States and other global actors help satisfy whatever concerns drove a state to want nuclear weapons in the first place. Governments typically pursue nuclear power for one of three reasons: to protect themselves against an external security threat, to satisfy the parochial interests of domestic actors, or to acquire an important status symbol. Iran is, mostly, a classic case of a state that wants nuclear weapons to dissuade an attack. It sits in a perennially unstable region, has long faced a belligerent Iraq, and now wants to stand up to Washington's calls for regime change in Tehran. Any viable solution to Tehran's appetite for nuclear weapons will therefore require that Washington learn to coexist peacefully with Iran's deeply problematic government. U.S. officials should not assume that Iran will go nuclear no matter what and draw up plans for containing it when it does. Nor should Washington rely exclusively on UN sanctions, which might not work. Instead, the U.S. government must dig into its diplomatic toolbox and offer—in conjunction with China, Russia, and the EU-3 (France, Germany, and the United Kingdom)—contingent security guarantees to Tehran.

DELUSIONS OF DETERRENCE

THE NUCLEAR monopoly the United States enjoyed at the end of World War II did not last long. Nonproliferation discussions in the United Nations soon after the war came to naught because the Soviet Union understandably distrusted any plan that gave the United States a monopoly on the scientific knowledge and engineering experience needed to build a nuclear weapon. As Cold War hostilities grew, first President Harry Truman and then President Dwight Eisenhower considered launching attacks against the Soviet Union to prevent it from developing a nuclear arsenal. Moscow had tested its first atomic bomb in 1949, but it was the prospect of the Soviets' amassing a large H-bomb arsenal that particularly alarmed Eisenhower. In 1953, he asked Secretary of State John Foster Dulles if "our duty to future generations did not require us to initiate war at the most propitious time that we could designate." Eisenhower eventually rejected the idea, however, because he feared the Red Army would respond by invading U.S. allies in Europe. Even if the United States did emerge victorious from such a conflict, Eisenhower told his advisers in 1954, "the colossal job of occupying the territories of a defeated enemy would be far beyond the resources of the United States at the conclusion of this war."

As the Soviet nuclear arsenal expanded, it triggered a chain reaction. The United Kingdom and France raced to develop their own nuclear weapons (which they first detonated in 1952 and

1960, respectively), partly as an independent deterrent to Soviet aggression in Europe but also as a symbol of their continuing great-power status. That U.S. allies developed such capacities did not much concern Washington, but the U.S. government became deeply worried that China under Mao Zedong might acquire its own bomb. Still, the Kennedy administration rejected plans to launch a preventive air strike on Chinese nuclear facilities in 1963 for fear that it would spark a major war and because the Soviets had rejected Washington's secret request for their assistance.

It is common today to look back nostalgically on those years as "the long peace." But this oversimplifies the challenges of the Cold War. Nuclear weapons did seem to have a sobering influence on the great powers, but that effect was neither automatic nor foolproof. Both the Soviet and the Chinese governments originally hoped that having the bomb would allow them to engage in more aggressive policies with impunity. Moscow repeatedly threatened West Berlin in the late 1950s and early 1960s, for example, confident that its growing arsenal would dissuade the United States from coming to West Germany's defense. Soviet Premier Nikita Khrushchev also believed that if the Soviet Union could place nuclear weapons in Cuba, the United States, once faced with the fait accompli, would be deterred by the Soviet arsenal from attacking Fidel Castro's regime.

What could be called dangerous learning by "trial and terror" also characterized relations with China. Mao appears to have genuinely believed that nuclear weapons were "paper tigers" and that China could survive any large-scale nuclear war. Beijing's foreign policy certainly did not turn moderate after its 1964 nuclear tests. Mao ordered military ambushes of Soviet armed forces on the disputed Chinese-Soviet border in March 1969, instructing Chinese generals not to worry about Moscow's response because "we, too, have atomic bombs." Soviet leaders retaliated against Chinese units along the border and threatened a preventive nuclear strike against China's nuclear facilities. Mao eventually accepted a negotiated settlement of the territorial dispute, but only after evacuating the Chinese leadership to the countryside and putting China's nuclear arsenal on alert.

THE FRIGHTENING crises of the 1960s led U.S. and Soviet leaders to understand that nuclear weapons guaranteed only a precarious peace. Increasingly, the two superpowers pursued bilateral arms control measures—such as the Strategic Arms Limitation Talks and the Anti-Ballistic Missile Treaty—to try to manage their nuclear relationship. They also recognized that a new multilateral approach was needed to stop the spread of nuclear weapons.

In March 1963, President John F. Kennedy told the press that he was "haunted" by the fear that by the 1970s the United States would "face a world in which 15 or 20 or 25 nations" possessed nuclear weapons. Five years of negotiations later, the United States, the Soviet Union, the United Kingdom, and 59 non-nuclear-weapons states signed the NPT. Under the terms of the treaty, states possessing nuclear weapons agreed not to transfer weapons or knowledge about how to build them to their friends and allies. (This commitment effectively ended Washington's hope of supplying West Germany and other NATO powers with "a multilateral force" of nuclear weapons, a prospect that had deeply troubled Moscow.) They also undertook "to work in good faith" toward the eventual elimination of nuclear weapons. The non-nuclear-weapons states, for their part, agreed not to seek nuclear weapons and to cooperate with inspectors from the International Atomic Energy Agency (IAEA) to allow monitoring of their peaceful nuclear research and energy facilities. The idea behind this "I won't if you won't" provision was to reduce the security threats, potential or real, that non-nuclear-weapons states posed to one another. The treaty also guaranteed that non-nuclear-weapons states in good standing would gain the full benefits of peaceful nuclear energy production, creating a "sovereign right," Iran has since argued, for any such state to develop a full nuclear-fuel production cycle of its own. The broad ambition behind the NPT was to slow down proliferation by reducing the demand for nuclear weapons. By both providing some assurance that states subscribing to the treaty would not develop nuclear bombs and creating, through the IAEA, a system to detect their efforts if they did, the NPT assuaged the security concerns of many states. It also reduced the bomb's appeal as a status symbol by creating an international norm according to which "responsible" states followed NPT commitments and only "rogue" states did not. And by offering hope that the nuclear states would take significant steps toward eventual disarmament, the treaty made it easier for nonnuclear governments to justify their own self-restraint to their domestic constituencies.

The NPT system proved reasonably successful for quite a long while. Although they are less discussed than the failures, the non-proliferation successes—the nuclear dogs that did not bark—are more numerous. Many non-nuclear-weapons states did continue to develop nuclear energy facilities after the NPT was signed, and some—such as Japan, with its massive plutonium stockpile—kept nuclear materials and continued their nuclear research in case the NPT regime fell apart. (Uncertainty about the treaty was so strong at first that Japan and other nonnuclear states insisted that they be allowed to review and renew their membership every five years.) But the NPT and U.S. security guarantees eventually reduced those countries' interest in proliferation. Other U.S. allies were caught cheating—most notably South Korea in the 1970s and Taiwan in the 1980s—but they ended suspected military-related activities when Washington confronted them and threatened to withdraw its security assistance. Egypt sought nuclear weapons in the early 1960s, but it signed the NPT in 1968 and ratified it in 1979 after striking a peace deal with Israel that reduced its national security concerns. Belarus, Kazakhstan, and Ukraine were nuclear powers from the moment of their independence, having inherited arsenals when the Soviet Union collapsed in 1991. But they soon handed over the weapons to Russia in exchange for economic assistance, highly limited security assurances from the United States, and a chance to join the NPT in good standing.

The NPT has been enough of a success that at the 1995 NPT Review Conference, all 178 states that had ratified it agreed to extend it permanently.

PERILS OF PROLIFERATION

A FEW outliers have bucked the system, however, and it is their actions that have bred the fatalism about proliferation that now dominates in Washington. Israel has never officially admitted to possessing nuclear weapons, but it is widely known to have constructed (with France's help) a small arsenal in the 1970s. South Africa secretly built seven nuclear devices under the apartheid regime in the 1980s (but unilaterally destroyed them well before a black-majority-rule government took over in 1994). India and Pakistan developed nuclear capabilities in the late 1980s and came out of the closet with them in May 1998. Iraq had been inching along, too, and after the 1981 Israeli air strike on its Osirak reactor, it started an underground gaseous diffusion facility to produce bomb-grade uranium, which was belatedly discovered and destroyed by UN inspectors after the 1991 Gulf War.

A number of political and military developments since the 1990s have further weakened the nonproliferation regime. The Pakistani scientist A. Q. Khan, among others, began secretly selling uranium-enrichment capabilities and even bomb designs to potential proliferators. The emergence of new nuclear states has threatened those states' neighbors, and the United States itself is increasingly seen as a security threat by some potential proliferators. Some states—Iran in particular—insist that they have a "right" to develop nuclear-fuel-production capabilities, which would get them uncomfortably close to developing nuclear bombs if they were subsequently to quit the treaty. In 1999, the U.S. Senate also dealt the regime a blow by voting against ratification of the Comprehensive Test Ban Treaty despite the Clinton administration's promise to ratify it during the 1995 NPT conference as proof of the U.S. commitment to eventual disarmament.

Most important, some new nuclear states have proved to be particularly risky actors. Consider the unsettling case of Pakistan. Islamabad has been dangerously lax since its 1998 nuclear tests, exercising weak control over its military personnel, intelligence officials, and scientists who have access to nuclear weapons, materials, and technology. Soon after the 1998 tests, Pakistani military planners developed more belligerent strategies against India. Dusting off an old plan, in the winter of 1999, Pakistani infantry units disguised as mujahideen snuck into Indian-held Kashmir. The incursion sparked the 1999 Kargil War, in which over 1,000 soldiers were killed on both sides before Pakistani forces reluctantly withdrew. According to U.S. and Indian intelligence, before the fighting ended, the Pakistani military had started to ready its nuclear-capable missiles for potential use. But when President Bill Clinton raised the possibility that this had happened with Pakistani Prime Minister Nawaz Sharif, he displayed a disturbing lack of knowledge about what his own military was doing. Similarly, Pakistani leaders gave important nuclear command-and-control responsibilities to the notorious Inter-Services Intelligence (ISI), which has intimate ties to both the Taliban and jihadist groups fighting in Kashmir. Doing so was a recipe for trouble, raising the risks that a rogue faction could steal a weapon or give it to terrorists. According to credible reports, during the Kargil War, Pakistani military planners and the ISI considered hiding Pakistan's nuclear weapons in western Afghanistan to protect them from a potential preemptive attack by India; they even contacted Taliban officials to explore the option. Islamabad has also exercised incredibly loose control over Pakistani nuclear scientists. After the 9/11 attacks, it was discovered that a number of individual scientists—including Sultan Bashiruddin Mahmood, a senior official of the Pakistan Atomic Energy Commission (PAEC)—had met with Osama bin Laden in Afghanistan and discussed techniques for developing nuclear weapons and other weapons of mass destruction. In April 2002, Pakistani President Pervez Musharraf admitted that PAEC scientists had been in contact with al Qaeda but claimed that "the scientists involved had only very superficial knowledge." Most proliferation experts also believe that senior Pakistani military officers were involved in many, if not all, of the deals in which A. Q. Khan and his associates sold nuclear centrifuge components to Iran and Libya, offered to help Saddam Hussein build a bomb just before the 1991 Gulf War, and provided North Korea with uranium-enrichment technology.

THE MOST DANGEROUS GAME

DEALING WITH a nuclear Iran in the near future would be more like dealing with Pakistan than with nuclearized democracies such as Israel and India or even nuclear totalitarian states such as the Soviet Union and China. Not only does Iranian President Mahmoud Ahmadinejad spew belligerent anti-Israel and Holocaust-denying statements, but the Iranian government as a whole continues to nurture revolutionary ambitions toward Iran's conservative Sunni neighbors and to support Hezbollah and other terrorist organizations. Tehran, like Islamabad, would be unlikely to maintain centralized control over its nuclear weapons or materials. In order to deter Tehran from giving nuclear weapons to terrorists, in January 2006 the French government announced that it would respond to nuclear terrorism with a nuclear strike of its own against any state that had served as the terrorists' accomplice. But this "attribution deterrence" posture glosses over the difficult question of what to do if the source of nuclear materials for a terrorist bomb is uncertain. It also ignores the possibility that Tehran, once in possession of nuclear weapons, would feel emboldened to engage in aggressive naval actions against tankers in the Persian Gulf or to assist terrorist attacks as it did with the Hezbollah bombing of the U.S. barracks at the Khobar Towers in Saudi Arabia in 1996.

There is no reason to assume that, even if they wanted to, central political authorities in Tehran could completely control the details of nuclear operations by the Islamic Revolutionary Guard Corps. The IRGC recruits young "true believers" to join its ranks, subjects them to ideological indoctrination (but not psychological-stability testing), and—as the IAEA discovered when it inspected Iran's centrifuge facilities in 2003—gives IRGC units responsibility for securing production sites for nuclear materials. The IRGC is known to have ties to terrorist organizations, which means that Iran's nuclear facilities, like its chemical weapons programs, are under the ostensible control of the organization that manages Tehran's contacts with foreign terrorists. It is misguided simply to hope that eventual regime change in Tehran would end the nuclear danger because, in the words of one Bush administration official, who spoke to *The New York Times* anonymously, Washington would then "have a different relationship with a different Iranian government." This wish assumes that another Iranian revolution would end gently, with an orderly transfer of power, rather than in chaos and with the control of nuclear weapons left unclear.

THE REASONS WHY

IF IRAN must not be allowed to go nuclear, what then can be done to stop it? A U.S. military strike on Iran today should be avoided for the same prudent reasons that led Eisenhower and Kennedy to choose diplomacy and arms control over preventive war in their dealings with the Soviet Union and China. Even if U.S. intelligence services were confident that they had identified all major nuclear-related sites in Iran (they are not) and the Pentagon could hit all the targets, the United States would expose itself (especially its bases in the Middle East and U.S troops in Afghanistan and Iraq), and its allies, to the possibility of severe retaliation. When asked about possible U.S. air strikes in August 2004, Iranian Defense Minister Ali Shamkhani said, "You may be surprised to know that the U.S. military presence near us is not power for the United States because this power may under certain circumstances become a hostage in our hands. . . . The United States is not the only power present in the region. We are also present from Khost to Kandahar in Afghanistan and we are present in the Gulf and can be present in Iraq." Iran might also support attacks by terrorist groups in Europe or the United States. Bush administration officials have sought to give some teeth to the threat of a military attack by hinting that Israel might strike on Washington's behalf. The Pentagon notified Congress in April 2005 of its intention to sell conventional GBU-28 "bunker-buster" bombs to Israel, and President George W. Bush reasserted Washington's commitment to "support Israel if her security is threatened." But an Israeli air strike on Iran's nuclear facilities would do no more good than a U.S. one: it could not destroy all the facilities and thus would leave Tehran to resume its uranium-enrichment program at surviving sites and would give Iran strong incentives to retaliate against U.S. forces in the Middle East. Muslim sentiment throughout the world would be all the more inflamed, encouraging terrorist responses against the West.

With no viable military option at hand, the only way for Washington to move forward is to give Tehran good reason to relinquish its pursuit of nuclear weapons. That, in turn, requires understanding why Tehran wants them in the first place. Iran's nuclear energy program began in the 1960s under the shah, but even he wanted to create a breakout option to get the bomb quickly if necessary. One of his senior energy advisers once recalled, "The shah told me that he does not want the bomb yet, but if anyone in the neighborhood has it, we must be ready to have it." At first, Ayatollah Ruhollah Khomeini objected to nuclear weapons and other weapons of mass destruction on religious grounds, but the mullahs abandoned such restraint after Saddam ordered chemical attacks on Iranian forces during the Iran-Iraq War. As former Iranian President Hashemi Rafsanjani, then the speaker of Iran's Parliament, noted in 1988, the conflict with Saddam showed that "the moral teachings of the world are not very effective when war reaches a serious stage," and so Iranians must "fully equip ourselves in the defensive and offensive use of chemical, bacteriological, and radiological weapons." Tehran began purchasing centrifuge components from A. Q. Khan's network in 1987 and received, according to the IAEA, documents on how to cast enriched uranium into the form needed for nuclear weapons. Iran's nuclear-development efforts were further accelerated when, after the 1991 Gulf War, UN inspectors discovered and disclosed that Iraq had been just one or two years away from developing nuclear weapons of its own.

The end of Saddam's rule in 2003 significantly reduced the security threat to Tehran. But by then the United States had already taken Iraq's place, Washington having made it clear that it wanted regime change in Iran, too. In his January 2002 State of the Union address, President Bush had denounced the governments of Iran, Iraq, and North Korea as members of an "axis of evil" with ties to international terrorism. Increasingly, Bush administration spokespeople were advocating "preemption" to counter proliferation. After the fall of Baghdad, an unidentified senior U.S. official told a *Los Angeles Times* reporter that Tehran should "take a number," hinting that it was next in line for regime change. It did not help that the 2002 Nuclear Posture Review, which was leaked to the press, listed Iran as one of the states to be considered as a potential target by U.S. nuclear war planners. When asked, in April 2006, whether the Pentagon was considering a potential preventive nuclear strike against Iranian nuclear facilities, President Bush pointedly replied, "All options are on the table."

In the meantime, Iran's program has advanced. The last official U.S. intelligence estimate given to Congress, in February 2006, vaguely stated that if Iran "continues on its current path. . . [it] will likely have the capacity to produce a nuclear weapon within the next decade"—an estimate that has since been widely interpreted to mean five to ten years. Last April, Tehran began operating a cascade of 164 uranium-enrichment centrifuges at Natanz. According to the State Department, it will take over 13 years for an experimental cascade of this size to produce enough highly enriched uranium for even a single nuclear weapon. But without an arms control agreement, Iran is free to construct more centrifuge cascades at Natanz, and without intrusive IAEA inspections in place, Iran could build a covert enrichment facility elsewhere. What was once a proliferation problem is now a proliferation crisis.

AGREED FRAMEWORK IN FARSI

THE DEPTH of Tehran's security concerns is precisely the reason that, despite the Bush administration's hopes, Libya cannot be a model for how to deal with Iran now. Libyan President Muammar al-Qaddafi finally relinquished the pursuit of nuclear weapons in 2003 in exchange for both an end to trade sanctions and positive economic incentives. But Tripoli was always a very different foe from Tehran. For one thing, the Libyans turned out to be the gang that could not proliferate straight. For years, Qaddafi reportedly tried but failed to purchase complete nuclear weapons directly from China, India, and Pakistan. When he did purchase 20 centrifuges and components for another 200 from A. Q. Khan in 1997, he could not get enough of the machines assembled in the right way. In the late 1990s, moreover, as Qaddafi's regime was becoming more concerned with domestic threats—economic stagnation and the rise of jihadist insurgents—than it was with external ones, its nuclear program began to turn into a liability. Tehran today is in a very different position: it is much closer to being able to develop weapons, and it continues to have serious external security reasons for wanting them.

A better source of inspiration for handling Iran would be the 1994 Agreed Framework that the United States struck with North Korea. The Bush administration has severely criticized the deal, but it contained several elements that could prove useful for solving the Iranian nuclear crisis.

After the North Koreans were caught violating their NPT commitments in early 1993 (they were covertly removing nuclear materials from the Yongbyon reactor), they threatened to withdraw from the treaty. Declaring that "North Korea cannot be allowed to develop a nuclear bomb," President Clinton threatened an air strike on the Yongbyon reactor site if the North Koreans took further steps to reprocess plutonium. In June 1994, as the Pentagon was reinforcing military units on the Korean Peninsula and briefing Clinton on war preparations, Pyongyang froze its plutonium production, agreed to let IAEA inspectors monitor the reactor site, and entered into bilateral negotiations with a view to eventually eliminating its nuclear capability. It is unclear whether North Korea blinked out of fear of military intervention, because of concerns about economic sanctions, or because Washington's proposal held out the promise of security guarantees and normalized relations. But the talks produced the October 1994 Agreed Framework, under which North Korea agreed to eventually dismantle its reactors, remain in the NPT, and implement full IAEA safeguards. In exchange, the United States promised to provide it with limited oil supplies, construct two peaceful light-water reactors for energy production, "move toward full normalization of political and economic relations," and extend "formal assurances to [North Korea] against the threat or use of nuclear weapons by the U.S."

By 2002, however, the Agreed Framework had broken down, not only because Pyongyang was suspected of cheating but also because it believed that the United States, by delaying construction of the light-water reactors and failing to start normalizing relations, had not honored its side of the bargain. When confronted with evidence of its secret uranium program, in November 2002, Pyongyang took advantage of the fact that the U.S. military was tied down in preparations for the invasion of Iraq and withdrew from the NPT, kicked out the inspectors, and started reprocessing plutonium. Pyongyang is now thought to have six to eight nuclear weapons, to be producing more plutonium in the Yongbyon reactor, and to be constructing a larger one.

President Bush famously promised, in his 2002 State of the Union address, that the United States "will not permit the world's most dangerous regimes to threaten us with the world's most destructive weapons." Yet when North Korea kicked out the IAEA inspectors, Secretary of State Colin Powell proclaimed that the situation was "not a crisis," and Bush repeatedly declared that the United States had "no intention of invading North Korea." Deputy Secretary of State Richard Armitage quickly underscored the position: "The president has no hostile intentions and no plans to invade. That's an indication that North Korea can have the regime that [it] want[s] to have." The point was not lost on Tehran.

The 1994 Agreed Framework thus serves as a reminder of what to do, and its failure as a warning about what to avoid. If Washington is to offer security assurances to Tehran, it would be wise to do so soon (making the assurances contingent on Tehran's not developing nuclear weapons), rather than offering them too late, as it did with North Korea (and thus making them contingent on Tehran's getting rid of any existing nuclear weapons). As with North Korea, any deal with Iran must be structured in a series of steps, each offering a package of economic benefits (light-water reactors, aircraft parts, or status at the World Trade Organization) in exchange for constraints placed on Iran's future nuclear development.

Both Washington and Tehran will need to make major compromises. The Bush administration has said that a condition of any deal must be that "not a single centrifuge can spin" in Iran. But it might have to soften its stance. Allowing Tehran to maintain its experimental 164-centrifuge cascade, which poses no immediate danger and yet is an important status symbol for the Iranian regime, could help Tehran save face and sell a deal with Washington to its domestic constituencies by allowing it to claim that the arrangement protects Iran's "sovereign right" to have a full nuclear fuel cycle. One way to do this would be to draw a line between research on uranium enrichment (which would be allowed) and significant production of enriched uranium (which would be prohibited). In exchange, Tehran would have to accept verifiable safeguards on all its enrichment operations, permit throughout the country the more intrusive type of inspections required by the Additional Protocol of the IAEA, supply the IAEA with full documentation about suspected past violations, and freeze the construction of more centrifuges and heavy-water reactors that could produce plutonium.

History, particularly that of U.S.–North Korean relations, suggests that such agreements are just the start of serious negotiations. Even if a deal is struck, delays and backsliding should be expected. To limit their impact and keep them from leading to the agreement's dissolution, it would be necessary for Washington to both keep its promises and maintain credible threats that it would impose sanctions or even use limited force against Iran if Tehran violated its commitments.

Most important, however, would be a reduction in the security threat that the United States poses to Iran. Given the need for Washington to have a credible deterrent against, say, terrorist attacks sponsored by Iran, it would be ill advised to offer Tehran a blanket security guarantee. But more limited guarantees, such as a commitment not to use nuclear weapons and other commitments of the type offered North Korea under the Agreed Framework, could be effective today. They would reassure Tehran and pave the way toward the eventual normalization of U.S.-Iranian relations while signaling to other states that nuclear weapons are not the be all and end all of security. None of this will happen, however, if U.S. officials keep threatening to topple the Iranian government. In any final settlement, Tehran will need to agree to freeze its nuclear program and end its support for terrorism, and Washington—along with China, Russia, and the EU-3—must issue a joint security guarantee that respects Iran's political sovereignty, thus committing the United States to promote democracy only by peaceful means. Peaceful coexistence does not require friendly relations, but it does mean exercising mutual restraint. Relinquishing the threat of regime change by force is a necessary and acceptable price for the United States to pay to stop Tehran from getting the bomb.⊕

Botching the Bomb

Why Nuclear Weapons Programs Often Fail on Their Own—and Why Iran's Might, Too

Jacques E. C. Hymans

Foreign Affairs, May/June 2012

THE CHRONIC problem of nuclear proliferation is once again dominating the news. A fierce debate has developed over how to respond to the threat posed by Iran's nuclear activities, which most experts believe are aimed at producing a nuclear weapon or at least the capacity to assemble one. In this debate, one side is pushing for a near-term military attack to damage or destroy Iran's nuclear program, and the other side is hoping that strict sanctions against the Islamic Republic will soften it up for a diplomatic solution. Both sides, however, share the underlying assumption that unless outside powers intervene in a dramatic fashion, it is inevitable that Iran will achieve its supposed nuclear goals very soon.

Yet there is another possibility. The Iranians had to work for 25 years just to start accumulating uranium enriched to 20 percent, which is not even weapons grade. The slow pace of Iranian nuclear progress to date strongly suggests that Iran could still need a very

JACQUES E. C. HYMANS is Associate Professor of International Relations at the University of Southern California. His most recent book is *Achieving Nuclear Ambitions: Scientists, Politicians, and Proliferation* (Cambridge University Press, 2012), from which this essay is adapted.

long time to actually build a bomb—or could even ultimately fail to do so. Indeed, global trends in proliferation suggest that either of those outcomes might be more likely than Iranian success in the near future. Despite regular warnings that proliferation is spinning out of control, the fact is that since the 1970s, there has been a persistent slowdown in the pace of technical progress on nuclear weapons projects and an equally dramatic decline in their ultimate success rate.

The great proliferation slowdown can be attributed in part to U.S. and international nonproliferation efforts. But it is mostly the result of the dysfunctional management tendencies of the states that have sought the bomb in recent decades. Weak institutions in those states have permitted political leaders to unintentionally undermine the performance of their nuclear scientists, engineers, and technicians. The harder politicians have pushed to achieve their nuclear ambitions, the less productive their nuclear programs have become. Meanwhile, military attacks by foreign powers have tended to unite politicians and scientists in a common cause to build the bomb. Therefore, taking radical steps to rein in Iran would be not only risky but also potentially counterproductive, and much less likely to succeed than the simplest policy of all: getting out of the way and allowing the Iranian nuclear program's worst enemies—Iran's political leaders—to hinder the country's nuclear progress all by themselves.

NUCLEAR DOGS THAT HAVE NOT BARKED

"TODAY, ALMOST any industrialized country can produce a nuclear weapon in four to five years," a former chief of Israeli military intelligence recently wrote in *The New York Times*, echoing a widely held belief. Indeed, the more nuclear technology and know-how have diffused around the world, the more the timeline for building a bomb should have shrunk. But in fact, rather than speeding up over the past four decades, proliferation has gone into slow motion.

Seven countries launched dedicated nuclear weapons projects before 1970, and all seven succeeded in relatively short order. By contrast, of the ten countries that have launched dedicated nuclear weapons projects since 1970, only three have achieved a bomb. And only one of the six states that failed—Iraq—had made much progress toward its ultimate goal by the time it gave up trying. (The jury is still out on Iran's program.) What is more, even the successful projects of recent decades have needed a long time to achieve their ends. The average timeline to the bomb for successful projects launched before 1970 was about seven years; the average timeline to the bomb for successful projects launched after 1970 has been about 17 years.

International security experts have been unable to convincingly explain this remarkable trend. The first and most credible conventional explanation is that the Nuclear Nonproliferation Treaty (NPT) has prevented a cascade of new nuclear weapons states by creating a system of export controls, technology safeguards, and onsite inspections of nuclear facilities. The NPT regime has certainly closed off the most straightforward pathways to the bomb. However, the NPT became a formidable obstacle to would-be nuclear states only in the 1990s, when its export-control lists were expanded and Western states finally became serious about enforcing them and when international inspectors started acting less like tourists and more like detectives. Yet the proliferation slowdown started at least 20 years before the system was solidified. So the NPT, useful though it may be, cannot alone account for this phenomenon.

A second conventional explanation is that although the NPT regime may not have been very effective, American and Israeli bombs have been. Syria's nascent nuclear effort, for instance, was apparently dealt a major setback by an Israeli air raid on its secret reactor construction site in 2007. But the record of military strikes is mixed. Contrary to the popular myth of the success of Israel's 1981 bombing of the Osiraq reactor in Iraq, the strike actually spurred Iraqi President Saddam Hussein to move beyond vague intentions and commit strongly to a dedicated nuclear weapons project, which lasted until the 1990–91 Gulf War. Moreover, the bombs that the United States dropped on Iraq during that conflict mostly missed Saddam's nuclear sites.

Finally, some analysts have asserted that nuclear weapons projects become inefficient due to political leaders' flagging levels of commitment. But these analysts are reversing cause and effect: leaders lose interest when their nuclear programs are not running well. And some nuclear weapons projects, such as France's, have performed well despite very tepid support from above. The imperfect correlation between the commitment of leaders and the quality of nuclear programs should not be surprising, for although commentators may speak casually of "Mao's bomb" or "Kim Jong Il's bomb," the real work has to be carried out by other people.

ARRESTED DEVELOPMENT

A MORE convincing explanation of the proliferation slowdown begins with the observation that during the early days of the nuclear age, most states with nuclear ambitions were in the developed world, whereas since the mid-1960s, most would-be nuclear states have been in the developing world. As proliferation has become a mainly developing-world phenomenon, timelines to the bomb have slowed down dramatically. But the relevant difference here is not primarily economic. Some nuclear programs in very poor states have fared rather well, such the one undertaken by famine-stricken China in the 1950s and 1960s. Conversely, wealthy oil states, such as Iraq and Libya, spent vast amounts on decades-long nuclear quests but still failed.

National income is only one dimension of development, however, and in this case it is not the most important one. As the political scientist Francis Fukuyama has stressed, despite strong rates of economic growth, most developing countries struggle to establish high-quality state bureaucracies. And a dysfunctional bureaucracy is likely to produce a dysfunctional nuclear weapons project.

Nuclear research and development organizations depend heavily on intense commitment, creative thinking, and a shared spirit of cooperation among large numbers of highly educated scientific and technical workers. To elicit this positive behavior, management needs to respect their professional autonomy and facilitate their efforts, and not simply order them around. Respect for professional autonomy was instrumental to the brilliant successes of the earliest nuclear weapons projects. Even in Stalin's Soviet Union, as the historian David Holloway has written, "it is striking how the apparatus of the police state fused with the physics community to build the bomb. . . . [The physics community's] autonomy was not destroyed by the creation of the nuclear project. It continued to exist within the administrative system that was set up to manage the project."

By contrast, most rulers of recent would-be nuclear states have tended to rely on a coercive, authoritarian management approach to advance their quest for the bomb, using appeals to scientists' greed and fear as the primary motivators. That coercive approach is a major mistake, because it produces a sense of alienation in the workers by removing their sense of professionalism. As a result, nuclear programs lose their way. Moreover, underneath these bad management choices lie bad management cultures. In developing states with inadequate civil service protections, every decision tends to become politicized, and state bureaucrats quickly learn to keep their heads down. Not even the highly technical matters faced by nuclear scientific and technical workers are safe from meddling politicians. The result is precisely the reverse of what the politicians intend: not heightened efficiency but rather a mixture of bureaucratic sloth, corruption, and endless blame shifting.

Although it is difficult to measure the quality of state institutions precisely, the historical record strongly indicates that the more a state has conformed to the professional management culture generally found in developed states, the less time it has needed to get its first bomb and the lower its chances of failure.

Conversely, the more a state has conformed to the authoritarian management culture typically found in developing states, the more time it has needed to get its first bomb and the higher its chances of failure.

Of course, not all developing states share the same model. For instance, as the political scientist Samuel Huntington famously argued, the Soviet Union's "bureaucratic" form of communism was merely a variation on the basic archetype of the western European state. Thus, although the Soviet Union was bad at many things, it was good at "big science." Likewise, China's successful nuclear weapons project took place at a time when the Chinese Communist Party was still clinging to the Soviet bureaucratic communist model, despite Chairman Mao Zedong's best efforts to wreck it. The Chinese nuclear program fared poorly when Mao was manhandling the party, but it fared well when the party was able to keep him at bay, which it managed to do just long enough to attain the bomb.

THE IRAQI NUCLEAR MIRAGE

THE CASE of Iraq's nuclear activities in the 1980s might seem to contradict the idea that the global proliferation slowdown has resulted from poor management practices. After all, according to the conventional wisdom in Washington, Iraq had come to within just a few months of obtaining its first bomb when the Gulf War serendipitously intervened. But in fact, the Iraqi case provides a clear instance of authoritarian mismanagement leading to an inefficient nuclear weapons project.

In the years leading up to Israel's 1981 attack on Iraq's half-built Osiraq reactor, Iraq's nuclear program had been ravaged by one of Saddam's periodic fits of peremptory dismissals and jailings of officials and scientists. But immediately after the strike, Saddam released Iraq's top nuclear scientist, Jafar Dhia Jafar, from house arrest and reinstalled him as the head of the nuclear program. (Jafar had been detained after objecting to the jailing of another top nuclear scientist.) Jafar's return marked the beginning of Iraq's dedicated nuclear weapons project. For a while, the project progressed well. The Israeli attack had awakened the nationalist pride of Iraq's nuclear scientists, and they were determined to succeed.

But in the mid-1980s, the program fell victim to a power grab by Hussein Kamel al-Majid, Saddam's powerful son-in-law. Kamel's reign over the nuclear program was almost a caricature of a coercive management approach. He imposed unrealistic deadlines for technical progress, causing machines and human beings alike to crack under the pressure. He pitted scientists against one another in brutal competition, forcing them to duplicate work that others had already completed. When progress toward the bomb appeared to stall, he demanded dramatic technical changes, rendering prior work practically meaningless. And his pursuit of sensitive materials on the international black market was so blatant that by the end of the 1980s, even the sleepiest nonproliferation watchdogs had begun to take notice.

Kamel relentlessly bullied his scientists, with predictable results. For instance, in 1987, he asked Mahdi Obeidi, the leader of the team tasked with building gas centrifuges, how long it would take to get the first one up and running. Obeidi imagined two years but, fearful of displeasing Kamel, said one year. In response, Kamel told Obeidi that he had 45 days. The result was a mad dash that caused the finely crafted, costly centrifuge rotor to crack on its first test run. Thanks to this rampant mismanagement, Iraq still had not produced any weapons-grade highly enriched uranium at all by the time the Gulf War intervened, even after spending $1 billion on ten years of work and despite successfully concealing the bulk of its program from the outside world. The Iraqi program was a "spectacular failure," according to Robert Kelley, a former inspector for the International Atomic Energy Agency (IAEA). "This was probably one of the most expensive undertakings in the history of mankind in terms of dollars spent to material produced."

After the Gulf War, international inspectors were shocked to find many large, well-equipped secret nuclear facilities in Iraq. With all that fancy equipment, Iraq probably could have built the bomb within a couple of years—if it had been able to count on a well-motivated, professional scientific and technical team. But by 1991, after years of coercive, authoritarian mismanagement, Iraq's scientific and technical workers had become exhausted, cynical, and divided. Most security analysts have been slow to understand this reality and have perpetuated the myth that Iraq was very close to building a bomb before the Gulf War.

Outside analysts have also overstated the threat posed by Iraq's "crash program," which was launched immediately after Saddam's 1990 invasion of Kuwait. The crash program was a last-ditch attempt to make a bomb with highly enriched uranium reactor fuel that Iraq had legally purchased under international safeguards in the late 1970s. In retrospect, those transfers should not have been permitted. But Iraq's management problems affected the crash program just as much as they affected every other aspect of the nuclear weapons project. As a result, even the crash program was badly stalled before the end of the Gulf War. Hence, from a strategic point of view, it did not matter that U.S. bombs missed Iraq's nuclear sites in 1991, because the Iraqi nuclear program had already crumbled from within.

CAVEAT EMPTOR

IRAQ'S EXPERIENCE notwithstanding, many proliferation analysts insist that although technologically backward states might not have been capable of nuclear weapons development in the past, they can now simply purchase all they need in the free-wheeling globalized marketplace. Admittedly, illicit nuclear entrepreneurs—such as A. Q. Khan, the rogue Pakistani scientist who sold nuclear technology to Iran, Libya, and North Korea—do pose a threat. But international nuclear technology transfers often fail because the dysfunctional states that are trying to get the bomb are hardly any better at exploiting foreign nuclear know-how than they are at developing their own.

Libya's misbegotten nuclear weapons project reflects this general pattern. Despite buying all the items in Khan's catalog, Libya was unable to "put them together and make them work," according to a 2005 U.S. government report. Indeed, when IAEA inspectors gained access to Libyan nuclear facilities after Libya's president, Muammar al-Qaddafi, abandoned the project in 2003, they found much of the imported merchandise still in its original packing crates.

As for some analysts' terrifying predictions of ex-Soviet nuclear scientists and technicians leaving home en masse to further the nuclear ambitions of rogue regimes, this is more the stuff of Hollywood than a genuine problem. Ex-Soviet researchers vastly prefer the professional establishments of the West over the secret lairs of brutal dictators. Moreover, developing-state rulers need to be wary of recruiting outsiders, since the few genuine nuclear experts available can be hard to distinguish from the scores of frauds and spies also on the market. Take, for instance, the case of Argentine President Juan Perón's post–World War II recruitment of Nazi scientists. This was perhaps the most successful effort to produce a reverse scientific brain drain in history. Yet Ronald Richter, the Austrian physicist whom Perón chose to head his nascent nuclear program, turned out to be part con man and part madman. Perón realized his error only after the snickering worldwide reaction to his 1951 announcement that Richter had succeeded in producing controlled fusion.

TARDY IN TEHRAN

IN THE intensifying crisis over Iran's nuclear activity, the great proliferation slowdown has gone all but unmentioned. Yet this robust global trend clearly indicates a need to guard against any hasty conclusion that Iran's nuclear program is about to achieve its ultimate aims. Iran's nuclear scientists and engineers may well find a way to inoculate themselves against Israeli bombs and computer hackers. But they face a potentially far greater obstacle in the form of Iran's long-standing authoritarian management culture. In a study of Iranian human-resource practices, the management analysts Pari Namazie and Monir Tayeb concluded that the Iranian regime has historically shown a marked preference for political loyalty over professional qualifications. "The belief," they wrote, "is that a loyal person can learn new skills, but it is much more difficult to teach loyalty to a skilled person." This is the classic attitude of authoritarian managers. And according to the Iranian political scientist Hossein Bashiriyeh, in recent years, Iran's "irregular and erratic economic policies and practices, political nepotism and general mismanagement" have greatly accelerated. It is hard to imagine that the politically charged Iranian nuclear program is sheltered from these tendencies.

It is surely more difficult to assess the quality of Iran's nuclear management than it is to count the number of Iranian centrifuge machines. But such an assessment is vital, because the progress of Iran's program will depend on how much professional autonomy its scientists and engineers are able to retain. In the meantime, a number of broad lessons from the great proliferation slowdown can help provide a more sober assessment of the situation.

The first lesson is to be wary of narrow, technocentric analyses of a state's nuclear weapons potential. Recent alarming estimates of Iran's timeline to the bomb have been based on the same assumptions that have led Israel and the United States to consistently overestimate Iran's rate of nuclear progress for the last 20 years. The majority of official U.S. and Israeli estimates during the 1990s predicted that Iran would acquire nuclear weapons by 2000. After that date passed with no Iranian bomb in sight, the estimate was simply bumped back to 2005, then to 2010, and most recently to 2015. The point is not that the most recent estimates are necessarily wrong but rather that they lack credibility. In particular, policymakers should heavily discount any intelligence assessments that do not explicitly account for the impact of management quality on Iran's proliferation timeline.

The second lesson of the proliferation slowdown is that policy-makers should reject analyses based on assumptions about a state's capacity to build nuclear programs in secret. Ever since the mid-1990s, official proliferation assessments have freely extrapolated from minimal data, a practice that led U.S. intelligence analysts to wrongly conclude that Iraq had reconstituted its weapons of mass destruction programs after the Gulf War. The United States must guard against the possibility of an equivalent intelligence failure over Iran. This is not to deny that Tehran may be keeping some of its nuclear work secret. But it is simply unreasonable to assume, for example, that Iran has compensated for the problems it has faced with centrifuges at the Natanz uranium-enrichment facility by hiding better-working centrifuges at some unknown facility. Indeed, when Iran has tried to hide weapons-related activities in the past, it has often been precisely because the work was at the very early stages or was going badly.

The third lesson is that states that poorly manage their nuclear programs can bungle even the supposedly easy steps of the process. For instance, based on estimates of the size of North Korea's plutonium stockpile and the presumed ease of weapons fabrication, U.S. intelligence agencies thought that by the 1990s, North Korea had built one or two nuclear weapons. But in 2006, North Korea's first nuclear test essentially fizzled, making it clear that the "hermit kingdom" did not have any working weapons at all. Even its second try, in 2009, did not work properly. Similarly, if Iran eventually does acquire a significant quantity of weapons-grade highly enriched uranium, this should not be equated with the possession of a nuclear weapon.

The fourth lesson is to avoid doing anything that might motivate scientific and technical workers to commit themselves more firmly to the nuclear weapons project. Nationalist fervor can partially compensate for poor organization. Therefore, violent actions, such as aerial bombardments or assassinations of scientists, are a loser's bet. As shown by the consequences of the Israeli attack on Osiraq, such strikes are liable to unite the state's scientific and technical workers behind their otherwise illegitimate political leadership. Acts of sabotage, such as the Stuxnet computer worm, which damaged Iranian nuclear equipment in 2010, stand at the extreme boundary between sanctions and violent attacks, and therefore they should be undertaken only after very thorough consideration.

Traditionally, nonproliferation strategy has revolved around persuading leaders to stop desiring nuclear weapons and depriving nuclear scientists of the tools necessary to build them. But scientists have motivations, too, and policymakers must keep in mind this critical third dimension of nuclear programs' efficiency. The world is lucky that during the past few decades, the leaders of would-be nuclear weapons states have been so good at frustrating and alienating their scientists. The United States and its partners must take care not to adopt policies that resolve those leaders' management problems for them.●

Time to Attack Iran

Why a Strike Is the Least Bad Option

Matthew Kroenig

Foreign Affairs, January/February 2012

IN EARLY October, U.S. officials accused Iranian operatives of planning to assassinate Saudi Arabia's ambassador to the United States on American soil. Iran denied the charges, but the episode has already managed to increase tensions between Washington and Tehran. Although the Obama administration has not publicly threatened to retaliate with military force, the allegations have underscored the real and growing risk that the two sides could go to war sometime soon—particularly over Iran's advancing nuclear program.

For several years now, starting long before this episode, American pundits and policymakers have been debating whether the United States should attack Iran and attempt to eliminate its nuclear facilities. Proponents of a strike have argued that the only thing worse than military action against Iran would be an Iran armed with nuclear weapons. Critics, meanwhile, have warned that such

MATTHEW KROENIG is Stanton Nuclear Security Fellow at the Council on Foreign Relations and the author of *Exporting The Bomb: Technology Transfer and the Spread of Nuclear Weapons.* From July 2010 to July 2011, he was a Special Adviser in the Office of the U.S. Secretary of Defense, responsible for defense strategy and policy on Iran.

a raid would likely fail and, even if it succeeded, would spark a full-fledged war and a global economic crisis. They have urged the United States to rely on nonmilitary options, such as diplomacy, sanctions, and covert operations, to prevent Iran from acquiring a bomb. Fearing the costs of a bombing campaign, most critics maintain that if these other tactics fail to impede Tehran's progress, the United States should simply learn to live with a nuclear Iran.

But skeptics of military action fail to appreciate the true danger that a nuclear-armed Iran would pose to U.S. interests in the Middle East and beyond. And their grim forecasts assume that the cure would be worse than the disease—that is, that the consequences of a U.S. assault on Iran would be as bad as or worse than those of Iran achieving its nuclear ambitions. But that is a faulty assumption. The truth is that a military strike intended to destroy Iran's nuclear program, if managed carefully, could spare the region and the world a very real threat and dramatically improve the long-term national security of the United States.

DANGERS OF DETERRENCE

YEARS OF international pressure have failed to halt Iran's attempt to build a nuclear program. The Stuxnet computer worm, which attacked control systems in Iranian nuclear facilities, temporarily disrupted Tehran's enrichment effort, but a report by the International Atomic Energy Agency this past May revealed that the targeted plants have fully recovered from the assault. And the latest IAEA findings on Iran, released in November, provided the most compelling evidence yet that the Islamic Republic has weathered sanctions and sabotage, allegedly testing nuclear triggering devices and redesigning its missiles to carry nuclear payloads. The Institute for Science and International Security, a nonprofit research institution, estimates that Iran could now produce its first nuclear weapon within six months of deciding to do so. Tehran's plans to move sensitive nuclear operations into more secure facilities over the course of the coming year could reduce the window for effective military action even further. If Iran expels IAEA inspectors, begins enriching its stockpiles of uranium to weapons-grade levels of 90 percent, or installs advanced centrifuges at its uranium-enrichment facility in Qom, the United States must strike immediately or forfeit its last opportunity to prevent Iran from joining the nuclear club.

Some states in the region are doubting U.S. resolve to stop the program and are shifting their allegiances to Tehran. Others have begun to discuss launching their own nuclear initiatives to counter a possible Iranian bomb. For those nations and the United States itself, the threat will only continue to grow as Tehran moves closer to its goal. A nuclear-armed Iran would immediately limit U.S. freedom of action in the Middle East. With atomic power behind it, Iran could threaten any U.S. political or military initiative in the Middle East with nuclear war, forcing Washington to think twice before acting in the region. Iran's regional rivals, such as Saudi Arabia, would likely decide to acquire their own nuclear arsenals, sparking an arms race. To constrain its geopolitical rivals, Iran could choose to spur proliferation by transferring nuclear technology to its allies—other countries and terrorist groups alike. Having the bomb would give Iran greater cover for conventional aggression and coercive diplomacy, and the battles between its terrorist proxies and Israel, for example, could escalate. And Iran and Israel lack nearly all the safeguards that helped the United States and the Soviet Union avoid a nuclear exchange during the Cold War—secure second-strike capabilities, clear lines of communication, long flight times for ballistic missiles from one country to the other, and experience managing nuclear arsenals. To be sure, a nuclear-armed Iran would not intentionally launch a suicidal nuclear war. But the volatile nuclear balance between Iran and Israel could easily spiral out of control as a crisis unfolds, resulting in a nuclear exchange between the two countries that could draw the United States in, as well.

These security threats would require Washington to contain Tehran. Yet deterrence would come at a heavy price. To keep the

Iranian threat at bay, the United States would need to deploy naval and ground units and potentially nuclear weapons across the Middle East, keeping a large force in the area for decades to come. Alongside those troops, the United States would have to permanently deploy significant intelligence assets to monitor any attempts by Iran to transfer its nuclear technology. And it would also need to devote perhaps billions of dollars to improving its allies' capability to defend themselves. This might include helping Israel construct submarine-launched ballistic missiles and hardened ballistic missile silos to ensure that it can maintain a secure second-strike capability. Most of all, to make containment credible, the United States would need to extend its nuclear umbrella to its partners in the region, pledging to defend them with military force should Iran launch an attack.

In other words, to contain a nuclear Iran, the United States would need to make a substantial investment of political and military capital to the Middle East in the midst of an economic crisis and at a time when it is attempting to shift its forces out of the region. Deterrence would come with enormous economic and geopolitical costs and would have to remain in place as long as Iran remained hostile to U.S. interests, which could mean decades or longer. Given the instability of the region, this effort might still fail, resulting in a war far more costly and destructive than the one that critics of a preemptive strike on Iran now hope to avoid.

A FEASIBLE TARGET

A NUCLEAR Iran would impose a huge burden on the United States. But that does not necessarily mean that Washington should resort to military means. In deciding whether it should, the first question to answer is if an attack on Iran's nuclear program could even work. Doubters point out that the United States might not know the location of Iran's key facilities. Given Tehran's previous attempts to hide the construction of such stations, most notably the uranium-enrichment facilities in Natanz and Qom, it is possible that the regime already possesses nuclear assets that a bombing campaign might miss, which would leave Iran's program damaged but alive.

This scenario is possible, but not likely; indeed, such fears are probably overblown. U.S. intelligence agencies, the IAEA, and opposition groups within Iran have provided timely warning of Tehran's nuclear activities in the past—exposing, for example, Iran's secret construction at Natanz and Qom before those facilities ever became operational. Thus, although Tehran might again attempt to build clandestine facilities, Washington has a very good chance of catching it before they go online. And given the amount of time it takes to construct and activate a nuclear facility, the scarcity of Iran's resources, and its failure to hide the facilities in Natanz and Qom successfully, it is unlikely that Tehran has any significant operational nuclear facilities still unknown to Western intelligence agencies.

Even if the United States managed to identify all of Iran's nuclear plants, however, actually destroying them could prove enormously difficult. Critics of a U.S. assault argue that Iran's nuclear facilities are dispersed across the country, buried deep underground and hardened against attack, and ringed with air defenses, making a raid complex and dangerous. In addition, they claim that Iran has purposefully placed its nuclear facilities near civilian populations, which would almost certainly come under fire in a U.S. raid, potentially leading to hundreds, if not thousands, of deaths.

These obstacles, however, would not prevent the United States from disabling or demolishing Iran's known nuclear facilities. A preventive operation would need to target the uranium-conversion plant at Isfahan, the heavy-water reactor at Arak, and various centrifuge-manufacturing sites near Natanz and Tehran, all of which are located aboveground and are highly vulnerable to air strikes. It would also have to hit the Natanz facility, which, although it is buried under reinforced concrete and ringed by air defenses, would not survive an attack from the U.S. military's new bunker-busting bomb, the 30,000-pound Massive Ordnance Penetrator, capable of penetrating up to 200 feet of reinforced concrete. The plant in Qom is built into the side of a mountain and thus represents a more challenging target. But the facility is not yet operational and still contains little nuclear equipment, so if the United States acted quickly, it would not need to destroy it.

Washington would also be able to limit civilian casualties in any campaign. Iran built its most critical nuclear plants, such as the one in Natanz, away from heavily populated areas. For those less important facilities that exist near civilian centers, such as the centrifuge-manufacturing sites, U.S. precision-guided missiles could pinpoint specific buildings while leaving their surroundings unscathed. The United States could reduce the collateral damage even further by striking at night or simply leaving those less important plants off its target list at little cost to the overall success of the mission. Although Iran would undoubtedly publicize any human suffering in the wake of a military action, the majority of the victims would be the military personnel, engineers, scientists, and technicians working at the facilities.

SETTING THE RIGHT REDLINES

THE FACT that the United States can likely set back or destroy Iran's nuclear program does not necessarily mean that it should. Such an attack could have potentially devastating consequences—for international security, the global economy, and Iranian domestic politics—all of which need to be accounted for.

To begin with, critics note, U.S. military action could easily spark a full-blown war. Iran might retaliate against U.S. troops or allies, launching missiles at military installations or civilian populations in the Gulf or perhaps even Europe. It could activate its proxies abroad, stirring sectarian tensions in Iraq, disrupting the Arab Spring, and ordering terrorist attacks against Israel and the United States. This could draw Israel or other states into the fighting and compel the United States to escalate the conflict in response. Powerful allies of Iran, including China and Russia, may attempt to economically and diplomatically isolate the United States. In the midst of such spiraling violence, neither side may see a clear path out of the battle, resulting in a long-lasting, devastating war, whose impact may critically damage the United States' standing in the Muslim world.

Those wary of a U.S. strike also point out that Iran could retaliate by attempting to close the Strait of Hormuz, the narrow access point to the Persian Gulf through which roughly 20 percent of the world's oil supply travels. And even if Iran did not threaten the strait, speculators, fearing possible supply disruptions, would bid up the price of oil, possibly triggering a wider economic crisis at an already fragile moment.

None of these outcomes is predetermined, however; indeed, the United States could do much to mitigate them. Tehran would certainly feel like it needed to respond to a U.S. attack, in order to reestablish deterrence and save face domestically. But it would also likely seek to calibrate its actions to avoid starting a conflict that could lead to the destruction of its military or the regime itself. In all likelihood, the Iranian leadership would resort to its worst forms of retaliation, such as closing the Strait of Hormuz or launching missiles at southern Europe, only if it felt that its very existence was threatened. A targeted U.S. operation need not threaten Tehran in such a fundamental way.

To make sure it doesn't and to reassure the Iranian regime, the United States could first make clear that it is interested only in destroying Iran's nuclear program, not in overthrowing the government. It could then identify certain forms of retaliation to which it would respond with devastating military action, such as attempting to close the Strait of Hormuz, conducting massive and sustained attacks on Gulf states and U.S. troops or ships, or launching terrorist attacks in the United States itself. Washington would then need to clearly articulate these "redlines" to Tehran during and after the attack to ensure that the message was not lost in battle. And it would need to accept the fact that it would have to absorb Iranian responses that fell short of these redlines without escalating the conflict. This might include accepting token missile strikes against U.S. bases and ships in the region—several salvos over the course of a few days that soon taper off—or the harassment of commercial and U.S. naval vessels. To avoid the kind of casualties that could compel the White House to escalate the struggle, the United States would need to evacuate nonessential personnel from U.S. bases within range of Iranian missiles and ensure that its troops were safely in bunkers before Iran launched its response. Washington might also need to allow for stepped-up support to Iran's proxies in Afghanistan and Iraq and missile and terrorist attacks against Israel. In doing so, it could induce Iran to follow the path of Iraq and Syria, both of which refrained from starting a war after Israel struck their nuclear reactors in 1981 and 2007, respectively.

Even if Tehran did cross Washington's redlines, the United States could still manage the confrontation. At the outset of any such violation, it could target the Iranian weapons that it finds most threatening to prevent Tehran from deploying them. To de-escalate the situation quickly and prevent a wider regional war, the United States could also secure the agreement of its allies to avoid responding to an Iranian attack. This would keep other armies, particularly the Israel Defense Forces, out of the fray. Israel should prove willing to accept such an arrangement in exchange for a U.S. promise to eliminate the Iranian nuclear threat. Indeed, it struck a similar agreement with the United States during the Gulf War, when it refrained from responding to the launching of Scud missiles by Saddam Hussein.

Finally, the U.S. government could blunt the economic consequences of a strike. For example, it could offset any disruption of oil supplies by opening its Strategic Petroleum Reserve and quietly encouraging some Gulf states to increase their production in the run-up to the attack. Given that many oil-producing nations in the region, especially Saudi Arabia, have urged the United States to attack Iran, they would likely cooperate.

Washington could also reduce the political fallout of military action by building global support for it in advance. Many countries may still criticize the United States for using force, but some—the Arab states in particular—would privately thank Washington for eliminating the Iranian threat. By building such a consensus in the lead-up to an attack and taking the outlined steps to mitigate it once it began, the United States could avoid an international crisis and limit the scope of the conflict.

ANY TIME IS GOOD TIME

CRITICS HAVE another objection: even if the United States managed to eliminate Iran's nuclear facilities and mitigate the consequences, the effects might not last long. Sure enough, there is no guarantee that an assault would deter Iran from attempting to rebuild its plants; it may even harden Iran's resolve to acquire nuclear technology as a means of retaliating or protecting itself in the future. The United States might not have the wherewithal or the political capital to launch another raid, forcing it to rely on the same ineffective tools that it now uses to restrain Iran's nuclear drive. If that happens, U.S. action will have only delayed the inevitable.

Yet according to the IAEA, Iran already appears fully committed to developing a nuclear weapons program and needs no further motivation from the United States. And it will not be able to simply resume its progress after its entire nuclear infrastructure is reduced to rubble. Indeed, such a devastating offensive could well force Iran to quit the nuclear game altogether, as Iraq did after its nuclear program was destroyed in the Gulf War and as Syria did after the 2007 Israeli strike. And even if Iran did try to reconstitute its nuclear program, it would be forced to contend with continued international pressure, greater difficulty in securing necessary nuclear materials on the international market, and the lurking possibility of subsequent attacks. Military action could, therefore, delay Iran's nuclear program by anywhere from a few years to a decade, and perhaps even indefinitely.

Skeptics might still counter that at best a strike would only buy time. But time is a valuable commodity. Countries often hope to delay worst-case scenarios as far into the future as possible in the hope that this might eliminate the threat altogether. Those countries whose nuclear facilities have been attacked—most recently Iraq and Syria—have proved unwilling or unable to restart their programs. Thus, what appears to be only a temporary setback to Iran could eventually become a game changer.

Yet another argument against military action against Iran is that it would embolden the hard-liners within Iran's government, helping them rally the population around the regime and eliminate any remaining reformists. This critique ignores the fact that the hard-liners are already firmly in control. The ruling regime has become so extreme that it has sidelined even those leaders once considered to be right-wingers, such as former President Ali Akbar Hashemi Rafsanjani, for their perceived softness. And Rafsanjani or the former presidential candidate Mir Hossein Mousavi would likely continue the nuclear program if he assumed power. An attack might actually create more openings for dissidents in the long term (after temporarily uniting Iran behind Ayatollah Ali Khamenei), giving them grounds for criticizing a government that invited disaster. Even if a strike would strengthen Iran's hard-liners, the United States must not prioritize the outcomes of Iran's domestic political tussles over its vital national security interest in preventing Tehran from developing nuclear weapons.

STRIKE NOW OR SUFFER LATER

ATTACKING IRAN is hardly an attractive prospect. But the United States can anticipate and reduce many of the feared consequences of such an attack. If it does so successfully, it can remove the incentive for other nations in the region to start their own atomic programs and, more broadly, strengthen global non-proliferation by demonstrating that it will use military force to prevent the spread of nuclear weapons. It can also head off a possible

Israeli operation against Iran, which, given Israel's limited capability to mitigate a potential battle and inflict lasting damage, would likely result in far more devastating consequences and carry a far lower probability of success than a U.S. attack. Finally, a carefully managed U.S. attack would prove less risky than the prospect of containing a nuclear-armed Islamic Republic—a costly, decades-long proposition that would likely still result in grave national security threats. Indeed, attempting to manage a nuclear-armed Iran is not only a terrible option but the worst.

With the wars in Afghanistan and Iraq winding down and the United States facing economic hardship at home, Americans have little appetite for further strife. Yet Iran's rapid nuclear development will ultimately force the United States to choose between a conventional conflict and a possible nuclear war. Faced with that decision, the United States should conduct a surgical strike on Iran's nuclear facilities, absorb an inevitable round of retaliation, and then seek to quickly de-escalate the crisis. Addressing the threat now will spare the United States from confronting a far more dangerous situation in the future.❸

Response

Not Time to Attack Iran

Why War Should Be a Last Resort

Colin H. Kahl

Foreign Affairs, March / April 2012

In "Time to Attack Iran" (January/February 2012), Matthew Kroenig takes a page out of the decade-old playbook used by advocates of the Iraq war. He portrays the threat of a nuclear-armed Iran as both grave and imminent, arguing that the United States has little choice but to attack Iran now before it is too late. Then, after offering the caveat that "attacking Iran is hardly an attractive prospect," he goes on to portray military action as preferable to other available alternatives and concludes that the United States can manage all the associated risks. Preventive war, according to Kroenig, is "the least bad option."

But the lesson of Iraq, the last preventive war launched by the United States, is that Washington should not choose war when there are still other options, and it should not base its decision to attack on best-case analyses of how it hopes the conflict will turn

Colin H. Kahl is an Associate Professor in the Security Studies Program at Georgetown University's Edmund A. Walsh School of Foreign Service and a Senior Fellow at the Center for a New American Security. In 2009–11, he was U.S. Deputy Assistant Secretary of Defense for the Middle East.

out. A realistic assessment of Iran's nuclear progress and how a conflict would likely unfold leads one to a conclusion that is the opposite of Kroenig's: now is not the time to attack Iran.

BAD TIMING

KROENIG ARGUES that there is an urgent need to attack Iran's nuclear infrastructure soon, since Tehran could "produce its first nuclear weapon within six months of deciding to do so." Yet that last phrase is crucial. The International Atomic Energy Agency (IAEA) has documented Iranian efforts to achieve the capacity to develop nuclear weapons at some point, but there is no hard evidence that Supreme Leader Ayatollah Ali Khamenei has yet made the final decision to develop them.

In arguing for a six-month horizon, Kroenig also misleadingly conflates hypothetical timelines to produce weapons-grade uranium with the time actually required to construct a bomb. According to 2010 Senate testimony by James Cartwright, then vice chairman of the U.S. Joint Chiefs of Staff, and recent statements by the former heads of Israel's national intelligence and defense intelligence agencies, even if Iran could produce enough weapons-grade uranium for a bomb in six months, it would take it at least a year to produce a testable nuclear device and considerably longer to make a deliverable weapon. And David Albright, president of the Institute for Science and International Security (and the source of Kroenig's six-month estimate), recently told Agence France-Presse that there is a "low probability" that the Iranians would actually develop a bomb over the next year even if they had the capability to do so. Because there is no evidence that Iran has built additional covert enrichment plants since the Natanz and Qom sites were outed in 2002 and 2009, respectively, any near-term move by Tehran to produce weapons-grade uranium would have to rely on its declared facilities. The IAEA would thus detect such activity with sufficient time for the international community to mount a forceful response. As a result, the Iranians are unlikely to commit to building nuclear weapons until they can do so much more quickly or out of sight, which could be years off.

Kroenig is also inconsistent about the timetable for an attack. In some places, he suggests that strikes should begin now, whereas in others, he argues that the United States should attack only if Iran takes certain actions—such as expelling IAEA inspectors, beginning the enrichment of weapons-grade uranium, or installing large numbers of advanced centrifuges—any one of which would signal that it had decided to build a bomb. Kroenig is likely right that these developments—and perhaps others, such as the discovery of new covert enrichment sites—would create a decision point for the use of force. But the Iranians have not taken these steps yet, and as Kroenig acknowledges, "Washington has a very good chance" of detecting them if they do.

RIDING THE ESCALATOR

KROENIG'S DISCUSSION of timing is not the only misleading part of his article; so is his contention that the United States could mitigate the "potentially devastating consequences" of a strike on Iran by carefully managing the escalation that would ensue. His picture of a clean, calibrated conflict is a mirage. Any war with Iran would be a messy and extraordinarily violent affair, with significant casualties and consequences.

According to Kroenig, Iran would not respond to a strike with its "worst forms of retaliation, such as closing the Strait of Hormuz or launching missiles at southern Europe" unless its leaders felt that the regime's "very existence was threatened." To mitigate this risk, he claims, the United States could "make clear that it is interested only in destroying Iran's nuclear program, not in overthrowing the government." But Iranian leaders have staked their domestic legitimacy on resisting international pressure to halt the nuclear program, and so they would inevitably view an attack on that program as an attack on the regime itself. Decades of hostility and perceived U.S. efforts to undermine the regime would reinforce this perception. And when combined with the emphasis on anti-Americanism in the ideology of the supreme leader and his hard-line advisers, as well as their general ignorance about what drives U.S. decision-making, this perception means that there is little prospect that Iranian leaders would believe that a U.S. strike had limited aims. Assuming the worst about Washington's intentions, Tehran is likely to overreact to even a surgical strike against its nuclear facilities.

Kroenig nevertheless believes that the United States could limit the prospects for escalation by warning Iran that crossing certain "redlines" would trigger a devastating U.S. counterresponse. Ironically, Kroenig believes that a nuclear-armed Iran would be deeply irrational and prone to miscalculation yet somehow maintains that under the same leaders, Iran would make clear-eyed decisions in the immediate aftermath of a U.S. strike. But the two countries share no direct and reliable channels for communication, and the inevitable confusion brought on by a crisis would make signaling difficult and miscalculation likely.

To make matters worse, in the heat of battle, Iran would face powerful incentives to escalate. In the event of a conflict, both sides would come under significant pressure to stop the fighting due to the impact on international oil markets. Since this would limit the time the Iranians would have to reestablish deterrence, they might choose to launch a quick, all-out response, without care for red-lines. Iranian fears that the United States could successfully disrupt its command-and-control infrastructure or preemptively destroy its ballistic missile arsenal could also tempt Iran to launch as many missiles as possible early in the war. And the decentralized nature of Iran's Islamic Revolutionary Guard Corps, especially its navy, raises the prospect of unauthorized responses that could rapidly expand the fighting in the crowded waters of the Persian Gulf.

Controlling escalation would be no easier on the U.S. side. In the face of reprisals by Iranian proxies, "token missile strikes against U.S. bases and ships," or "the harassment of commercial and U.S. naval vessels," Kroenig says that Washington should turn the other cheek and constrain its own response to Iranian counter-attacks. But this is much easier said than done. Just as Iran's likely expectation of a short war might encourage it to respond disproportionately early in the crisis, so the United States would also have incentives to move swiftly to destroy Iran's conventional forces and the infrastructure of the Revolutionary Guard Corps. And if the United States failed to do so, proxy attacks against U.S. civilian personnel in Lebanon or Iraq, the transfer of lethal rocket and portable air defense systems to Taliban fighters in Afghanistan, or missile strikes against U.S. facilities in the Gulf could cause significant U.S. casualties, creating irresistible political pressure in Washington to respond. Add to this the normal fog of war and the lack of reliable communications between the United States and Iran, and Washington would have a hard time determining whether Tehran's initial response to a strike was a one-off event or the prelude to a wider campaign. If it were the latter, a passive U.S. approach might motivate Iran to launch even more dangerous attacks—and this is a risk Washington may choose not to take. The sum total of these dynamics would make staying within Kroenig's proscribed limits exceedingly difficult.

Even if Iran did not escalate, purely defensive moves that would threaten U.S. personnel or international shipping in the Strait of Hormuz—the maritime chokepoint through which nearly 20 percent of the world's traded oil passes—would also create powerful incentives for Washington to preemptively target Iran's military. Of particular concern would be Iran's "anti-access/area-denial" capabilities, which are designed to prevent advanced navies from operating in the shallow waters of the Persian Gulf. These systems integrate coastal air defenses, shore-based long-range artillery and antiship cruise missiles, Kilo-class and midget submarines, remote-controlled boats and unmanned kamikaze aerial vehicles, and more than 1,000 small attack craft equipped with machine guns, multiple-launch rockets, antiship missiles, torpedoes, and rapid-mine-laying capabilities. The entire 120-mile-long strait sits along the Iranian coastline, within short reach of these systems. In the midst of a conflict, the threat to U.S. forces and the global economy posed by Iran's activating its air defenses, dispersing its missiles or naval forces, or moving its mines out of storage would be too great for the United States to ignore; the logic of preemption would compel Washington to escalate.

Some analysts, including Afshin Molavi and Michael Singh, believe that the Iranians are unlikely to attempt to close the strait due to the damage it would inflict on their own economy. But Tehran's saber rattling has already intensified in response to the prospect of Western sanctions on its oil industry. In the immediate aftermath of a U.S. strike on Iran's nuclear program, Iranian leaders might perceive that holding the strait at risk would encourage international pressure on Washington to end the fighting, possibly deterring U.S. escalation. In reality, it would more likely have the opposite effect, encouraging aggressive U.S. efforts to protect commercial shipping. The U.S. Navy is capable of keeping the strait open, but the mere threat of closure could send oil prices soaring, dealing a heavy blow to the fragile global economy. The measures that Kroenig advocates to mitigate this threat, such as opening up the U.S. Strategic Petroleum Reserve and urging Saudi Arabia to boost oil production, would be unlikely to suffice, especially since most Saudi crude passes through the strait.

Ultimately, if the United States and Iran go to war, there is no doubt that Washington will win in the narrow operational sense. Indeed, with the impressive array of U.S. naval and air forces already deployed in the Gulf, the United States could probably knock Iran's military capabilities back 20 years in a matter of weeks. But a U.S.-Iranian conflict would not be the clinical, tightly controlled, limited encounter that Kroenig predicts.

SPILLOVER

KEEPING OTHER states in the region out of the fight would also prove more difficult than Kroenig suggests. Iran would presume Israeli complicity in a U.S. raid and would seek to drag Israel into the conflict in order to undermine potential support for the U.S. war effort among key Arab regimes. And although it is true, as Kroenig notes, that Israel remained on the sidelines during the 1990–91 Gulf War, the threat posed by Iran's missiles and proxies today is considerably greater than that posed by Iraq two decades ago. If Iranian-allied Hezbollah responded to the fighting by firing rockets at Israeli cities, Israel could launch an all-out war against Lebanon. Syrian President Bashar al-Assad might also try to use the moment to divert attention from the uprising in his country, launching his own assault on the Jewish state. Either scenario, or their combination, could lead to a wider war in the Levant.

Even in the Gulf, where U.S. partners are sometimes portrayed as passive, Iranian retaliation might draw Saudi Arabia and the United Arab Emirates into the conflict. The Saudis have taken a much more confrontational posture toward Iran in the past year, and Riyadh is unlikely to tolerate Iranian attacks against critical energy infrastructure. For its part, the UAE, the most hawkish state in the Gulf, might respond to missiles raining down on U.S. forces at its Al Dhafra Air Base by attempting to seize Abu Musa, Greater Tunb, and Lesser Tunb, three disputed Gulf islands currently occupied by Iran.

A strike could also set off wider destabilizing effects. Although Kroenig is right that some Arab leaders would privately applaud a U.S. strike, many on the Arab street would reject it. Both Islamist extremists and embattled elites could use this opportunity to transform the Arab Spring's populist antiregime narrative into a decidedly anti-American one. This would rebound to Iran's advantage just at the moment when political developments in the region, chief among them the resurgence of nationalism in the Arab world and the upheaval in Syria, are significantly undermining Iran's influence. A U.S. strike could easily shift regional sympathies back in Tehran's favor by allowing Iran to play the victim and, through its retaliation, resuscitate its status as the champion of the region's anti-Western resistance.

THE COST OF BUYING TIME

EVEN IF a U.S. strike went as well as Kroenig predicts, there is little guarantee that it would produce lasting results. Senior U.S. defense officials have repeatedly stated that an attack on Iran's nuclear facilities would stall Tehran's progress for only a few years. Kroenig argues that such a delay could become permanent. "Those countries whose nuclear facilities have been attacked—most recently Iraq and Syria," he writes, "have proved unwilling or unable to restart their programs." In the case of Iraq, however, Saddam Hussein restarted his clandestine nuclear weapons program after the 1981 Israeli attack on the Osirak nuclear reactor, and it required the Gulf War and another decade of sanctions and intrusive inspections to eliminate it. Iran's program is also more advanced and dispersed than were Iraq's and Syria's, meaning it would be easier to reconstitute. A U.S. strike would damage key Iranian facilities, but it would do nothing to reverse the nuclear knowledge Iran has accumulated or its ability to eventually build new centrifuges.

A U.S. attack would also likely rally domestic Iranian support around nuclear hard-liners, increasing the odds that Iran would emerge from a strike even more committed to building a bomb. Kroenig downplays the "rally round the flag" risks by noting that hard-liners are already firmly in power and suggesting that an attack might produce increased internal criticism of the regime. But the nuclear program remains an enormous source of national pride for the majority of Iranians. To the extent that there is internal dissent over the program, it is a discussion about whether the country should acquire nuclear weapons or simply pursue civilian nuclear technology. By demonstrating the vulnerability of a non-nuclear-armed Iran, a U.S. attack would provide ammunition to hard-liners who argue for acquiring a nuclear deterrent. Kroenig suggests that the United States should essentially ignore "Iran's domestic political tussles" when pursuing "its vital national security interest in preventing Tehran from developing nuclear weapons." But influencing Iranian opinion about the strategic desirability of nuclear weapons might ultimately offer the only enduring way of keeping the Islamic Republic on a peaceful nuclear path.

Finally, if Iran did attempt to restart its nuclear program after an attack, it would be much more difficult for the United States to stop it. An assault would lead Iran to distance itself from the IAEA and perhaps to pull out of the Nuclear Non-proliferation Treaty altogether. Without inspectors on the ground, the international community would struggle to track or slow Tehran's efforts to rebuild its program.

CONTAIN YOURSELF

KROENIG ARGUES that "a nuclear-armed Iran would not intentionally launch a suicidal nuclear war" but still concludes that it is ultimately less risky to attack the Islamic Republic now than to attempt to contain it later. He warns that containment would entail a costly forward deployment of large numbers of U.S. forces on Iran's periphery for decades.

But the United States already has a large presence encircling Iran. Forty thousand U.S. troops are stationed in the Gulf, accompanied by strike aircraft, two aircraft carrier strike groups, two Aegis ballistic missile defense ships, and multiple Patriot antimissile systems. On Iran's eastern flank, Washington has another 90,000 troops deployed in Afghanistan and thousands more supporting the Afghan war in nearby Central Asian states. Kroenig claims that it would take much more to contain a nuclear-armed Iran. But U.S. forces in the Gulf already outnumber those in South Korea that are there to deter a nuclear-armed North. It is thus perfectly conceivable that the existing U.S. presence in the region, perhaps supplemented by a limited forward deployment of nuclear weapons and additional ballistic missile defenses, would be sufficient to deter a nuclear-armed Iran from aggression and blackmail.

To be sure, such a deterrence-and-containment strategy would be an extra-ordinarily complex and risky enterprise, and there is no doubt that prevention is preferable. Given the possible consequences of a nuclear-armed Iran, the price of failure would be very high. But

Kroenig's approach would not solve the problem. By presenting the options as either a near-term strike or long-term containment, Kroenig falls into the same trap that advocates of the Iraq war fell into a decade ago: ignoring postwar scenarios. In reality, the strike that Kroenig recommends would likely be a prelude to containment, not a substitute for it.

Since a military raid would not permanently eliminate Iran's nuclear infrastructure, the United States would still need to construct an expensive, risky postwar containment regime to prevent Iran from reconstituting the program, much as it did in regard to Iraq after the Gulf War. The end result would be strikingly similar to the one that Kroenig criticizes, requiring Washington to maintain sufficient air, naval, and ground forces in the Persian Gulf to attack again at a moment's notice.

A strike carried out in the way Kroenig advocates—a unilateral preventive attack—would also make postwar containment more difficult and costly. Many countries would view such an operation as a breach of international law, shattering the consensus required to maintain an effective poststrike containment regime. The likelihood that the United States could "reduce the political fallout of military action by building global support for it in advance," as Kroenig suggests, would be extremely low absent clear evidence that Iran is dashing for a bomb. Without such evidence, Washington would be left to bear the costs of an attack and the resulting containment regime alone.

Finally, the surgical nature of Kroenig's proposed strike, aimed solely at Iran's nuclear program, would make postwar containment much harder. It would leave Tehran wounded and aggrieved but still capable of responding. Kroenig's recommended approach, then, would likely be just enough to ensure a costly, long-term conflict without actually compelling Iran to change its behavior.

THE OPTIONS ON THE TABLE

IN MAKING the case for preventive war as the least bad option, Kroenig dismisses any prospect of finding a diplomatic solution to the U.S.-Iranian standoff. He concludes that the Obama administration's dual-track policy of engagement and pressure has failed to arrest Iran's march toward a bomb, leaving Washington with no other choice but to bomb Iran.

But this ignores the severe economic strain, isolation, and technical challenges that Iran is experiencing. After years of dismissing the economic effects of sanctions, senior Iranian officials now publicly complain about the intense pain the sanctions are producing. And facing the prospect of U.S. sanctions against Iran's central bank and European actions to halt Iranian oil imports, Tehran signaled in early January some willingness to return to the negotiating table. Washington must test this willingness and, in so doing, provide Iran with a clear strategic choice: address the concerns of the international community regarding its nuclear program and see its isolation lifted or stay on its current path and face substantially higher costs. In framing this choice, Washington must be able to assert that like-minded states are prepared to implement oil-related sanctions, and the Obama administration should continue to emphasize that all options, including military action, remain on the table.

Some will undoubtedly claim that highlighting the potential risks associated with war will lead the Iranians to conclude that the United States lacks the resolve to use force. But in authorizing the surge in Afghanistan, carrying out the raid that killed Osama bin Laden, and leading the NATO air campaign to oust Libya's Muammar al-Qaddafi, President Barack Obama has repeatedly shown that he is willing to accept risk and use force—both as part of a coalition and unilaterally—to defend U.S. interests. And as Martin Dempsey, chairman of the U.S. Joint Chiefs of Staff, told CNN late last December, the United States has a viable contingency plan for Iran if force is ultimately required. But given the high costs and inherent uncertainties of a strike, the United States should not rush to use force until all other options have been exhausted and the Iranian threat is not just growing but imminent. Until then, force is, and should remain, a last resort, not a first choice.

Why Iran Should Get the Bomb

Nuclear Balancing Would Mean Stability

Kenneth N. Waltz

Foreign Affairs, July / August 2012

THE PAST several months have witnessed a heated debate over the best way for the United States and Israel to respond to Iran's nuclear activities. As the argument has raged, the United States has tightened its already robust sanctions regime against the Islamic Republic, and the European Union announced in January that it will begin an embargo on Iranian oil on July 1. Although the United States, the EU, and Iran have recently returned to the negotiating table, a palpable sense of crisis still looms.

It should not. Most U.S., European, and Israeli commentators and policymakers warn that a nuclear-armed Iran would be the worst possible outcome of the current standoff. In fact, it would probably be the best possible result: the one most likely to restore stability to the Middle East.

POWER BEGS TO BE BALANCED

THE CRISIS over Iran's nuclear program could end in three different ways. First, diplomacy coupled with serious sanctions

KENNETH N. WALTZ is Senior Research Scholar at the Saltzman Institute of War and Peace Studies and Adjunct Professor of Political Science at Columbia University.

could convince Iran to abandon its pursuit of a nuclear weapon. But this outcome is unlikely: the historical record indicates that a country bent on acquiring nuclear weapons can rarely be dissuaded from doing so. Punishing a state through economic sanctions does not inexorably derail its nuclear program. Take North Korea, which succeeded in building its weapons despite countless rounds of sanctions and UN Security Council resolutions. If Tehran determines that its security depends on possessing nuclear weapons, sanctions are unlikely to change its mind. In fact, adding still more sanctions now could make Iran feel even more vulnerable, giving it still more reason to seek the protection of the ultimate deterrent.

The second possible outcome is that Iran stops short of testing a nuclear weapon but develops a breakout capability, the capacity to build and test one quite quickly. Iran would not be the first country to acquire a sophisticated nuclear program without building an actual bomb. Japan, for instance, maintains a vast civilian nuclear infrastructure. Experts believe that it could produce a nuclear weapon on short notice.

Such a breakout capability might satisfy the domestic political needs of Iran's rulers by assuring hard-liners that they can enjoy all the benefits of having a bomb (such as greater security) without the downsides (such as international isolation and condemnation). The problem is that a breakout capability might not work as intended.

The United States and its European allies are primarily concerned with weaponization, so they might accept a scenario in which Iran stops short of a nuclear weapon. Israel, however, has made it clear that it views a significant Iranian enrichment capacity alone as an unacceptable threat. It is possible, then, that a verifiable commitment from Iran to stop short of a weapon could appease major Western powers but leave the Israelis unsatisfied. Israel would be less intimidated by a virtual nuclear weapon than it would be by an actual one and therefore would likely continue its risky efforts at subverting Iran's nuclear program through sabotage and assassination—which could lead Iran to conclude that a breakout capability is an insufficient deterrent, after all, and that only weaponization can provide it with the security it seeks.

The third possible outcome of the standoff is that Iran continues its current course and publicly goes nuclear by testing a weapon. U.S. and Israeli officials have declared that outcome unacceptable, arguing that a nuclear Iran is a uniquely terrifying prospect, even an existential threat. Such language is typical of major powers, which have historically gotten riled up whenever another country has begun to develop a nuclear weapon of its own. Yet so far, every time another country has managed to shoulder its way into the nuclear club, the other members have always changed tack and decided to live with it. In fact, by reducing imbalances in military power, new nuclear states generally produce more regional and international stability, not less.

Israel's regional nuclear monopoly, which has proved remarkably durable for the past four decades, has long fueled instability in the Middle East. In no other region of the world does a lone, unchecked nuclear state exist. It is Israel's nuclear arsenal, not Iran's desire for one, that has contributed most to the current crisis. Power, after all, begs to be balanced. What is surprising about the Israeli case is that it has taken so long for a potential balancer to emerge.

Of course, it is easy to understand why Israel wants to remain the sole nuclear power in the region and why it is willing to use force to secure that status. In 1981, Israel bombed Iraq to prevent a challenge to its nuclear monopoly. It did the same to Syria in 2007 and is now considering similar action against Iran. But the very acts that have allowed Israel to maintain its nuclear edge in the short term have prolonged an imbalance that is unsustainable in the long term. Israel's proven ability to strike potential nuclear rivals with impunity has inevitably made its enemies anxious to develop the means to prevent Israel from doing so again. In this way, the current tensions are best viewed not as the early stages of a relatively recent Iranian nuclear crisis but rather as the final stages of a decades-long Middle East nuclear crisis that will end only when a balance of military power is restored.

UNFOUNDED FEARS

ONE REASON the danger of a nuclear Iran has been grossly exaggerated is that the debate surrounding it has been distorted by misplaced worries and fundamental misunderstandings of how states generally behave in the international system. The first prominent concern, which undergirds many others, is that the Iranian regime is innately irrational. Despite a widespread belief to the contrary, Iranian policy is made not by "mad mullahs" but by perfectly sane ayatollahs who want to survive just like any other leaders. Although Iran's leaders indulge in inflammatory and hateful rhetoric, they show no propensity for self-destruction. It would be a grave error for policymakers in the United States and Israel to assume otherwise.

Yet that is precisely what many U.S. and Israeli officials and analysts have done. Portraying Iran as irrational has allowed them to argue that the logic of nuclear deterrence does not apply to the Islamic Republic. If Iran acquired a nuclear weapon, they warn, it would not hesitate to use it in a first strike against Israel, even though doing so would invite massive retaliation and risk destroying everything the Iranian regime holds dear.

Although it is impossible to be certain of Iranian intentions, it is far more likely that if Iran desires nuclear weapons, it is for the purpose of providing for its own security, not to improve its offensive capabilities (or destroy itself). Iran may be intransigent at the negotiating table and defiant in the face of sanctions, but it still acts to secure its own preservation. Iran's leaders did not, for example, attempt to close the Strait of Hormuz despite issuing blustery warnings that they might do so after the EU announced its planned oil embargo in January. The Iranian regime clearly concluded that it did not want to provoke what would surely have been a swift and devastating American response to such a move.

Nevertheless, even some observers and policymakers who accept that the Iranian regime is rational still worry that a nuclear weapon would embolden it, providing Tehran with a shield that would allow it to act more aggressively and increase its support for terrorism. Some analysts even fear that Iran would directly provide terrorists with nuclear arms. The problem with these concerns is that they contradict the record of every other nuclear weapons state going back to 1945. History shows that when countries acquire the bomb, they feel increasingly vulnerable and become acutely aware that their nuclear weapons make them a potential target in the eyes of major powers. This awareness discourages nuclear states from bold and aggressive action. Maoist China, for example, became much less bellicose after acquiring nuclear weapons in 1964, and India and Pakistan have both become more cautious since going nuclear. There is little reason to believe Iran would break this mold.

As for the risk of a handoff to terrorists, no country could transfer nuclear weapons without running a high risk of being found out. U.S. surveillance capabilities would pose a serious obstacle, as would the United States' impressive and growing ability to identify the source of fissile material. Moreover, countries can never entirely control or even predict the behavior of the terrorist groups they sponsor. Once a country such as Iran acquires a nuclear capability, it will have every reason to maintain full control over its arsenal. After all, building a bomb is costly and dangerous. It would make little sense to transfer the product of that investment to parties that cannot be trusted or managed.

Another oft-touted worry is that if Iran obtains the bomb, other states in the region will follow suit, leading to a nuclear arms race in the Middle East. But the nuclear age is now almost 70 years old, and so far, fears of proliferation have proved to be unfounded. Properly defined, the term "proliferation" means a rapid and uncontrolled spread. Nothing like that has occurred; in fact, since 1970, there has been a marked slowdown in the emergence of nuclear states. There is no reason to expect that this pattern will change now. Should Iran become the second Middle Eastern nuclear power since 1945, it would hardly signal the start of a landslide. When Israel acquired the bomb in the 1960s, it was at war with many of its neighbors. Its nuclear arms were a much bigger threat to the Arab world than Iran's program is today. If an atomic Israel did not trigger an arms race then, there is no reason a nuclear Iran should now.

REST ASSURED

In 1991, the historical rivals India and Pakistan signed a treaty agreeing not to target each other's nuclear facilities. They realized that far more worrisome than their adversary's nuclear deterrent was the instability produced by challenges to it. Since then, even in the face of high tensions and risky provocations, the two countries have kept the peace. Israel and Iran would do well to consider this precedent. If Iran goes nuclear, Israel and Iran will deter each other, as nuclear powers always have. There has never been a full-scale war between two nuclear-armed states. Once Iran crosses the nuclear threshold, deterrence will apply, even if the Iranian arsenal is relatively small. No other country in the region will have an incentive to acquire its own nuclear capability, and the current crisis will finally dissipate, leading to a Middle East that is more stable than it is today.

For that reason, the United States and its allies need not take such pains to prevent the Iranians from developing a nuclear weapon. Diplomacy between Iran and the major powers should continue, because open lines of communication will make the Western countries feel better able to live with a nuclear Iran. But the current sanctions on Iran can be dropped: they primarily harm ordinary Iranians, with little purpose.

Most important, policymakers and citizens in the Arab world, Europe, Israel, and the United States should take comfort from the fact that history has shown that where nuclear capabilities emerge, so, too, does stability. When it comes to nuclear weapons, now as ever, more may be better.✿

After Iran Gets the Bomb

Containment and Its Complications

James M. Lindsay and Ray Takeyh

Foreign Affairs, March / April 2010

THE ISLAMIC Republic of Iran is determined to become the world's tenth nuclear power. It is defying its international obligations and resisting concerted diplomatic pressure to stop it from enriching uranium. It has flouted several UN Security Council resolutions directing it to suspend enrichment and has refused to fully explain its nuclear activities to the International Atomic Energy Agency. Even a successful military strike against Iran's nuclear facilities would delay Iran's program by only a few years, and it would almost certainly harden Tehran's determination to go nuclear. The ongoing political unrest in Iran could topple the regime, leading to fundamental changes in Tehran's foreign policy and ending its pursuit of nuclear weapons. But that is an outcome that cannot be assumed. If Iran's nuclear program continues to progress at its current rate, Tehran could have the nuclear material needed to build a bomb before U.S. President Barack Obama's current term in office expires.

The dangers of Iran's entry into the nuclear club are well known: emboldened by this development, Tehran might multiply its

---

JAMES M. LINDSAY is Senior Vice President, Director of Studies, and Maurice R. Greenberg Chair at the Council on Foreign Relations. RAY TAKEYH is a Senior Fellow at the Council on Foreign Relations and the author of *Guardians of the Revolution: Iran and the World in the Age of the Ayatollahs*.

attempts at subverting its neighbors and encouraging terrorism against the United States and Israel; the risk of both conventional and nuclear war in the Middle East would escalate; more states in the region might also want to become nuclear powers; the geopolitical balance in the Middle East would be reordered; and broader efforts to stop the spread of nuclear weapons would be undermined. The advent of a nuclear Iran—even one that is satisfied with having only the materials and infrastructure necessary to assemble a bomb on short notice rather than a nuclear arsenal— would be seen as a major diplomatic defeat for the United States. Friends and foes would openly question the U.S. government's power and resolve to shape events in the Middle East. Friends would respond by distancing themselves from Washington; foes would challenge U.S. policies more aggressively.

Such a scenario can be avoided, however. Even if Washington fails to prevent Iran from going nuclear, it can contain and mitigate the consequences of Iran's nuclear defiance. It should make clear to Tehran that acquiring the bomb will not produce the benefits it anticipates but isolate and weaken the regime. Washington will need to lay down clear "redlines" defining what it considers to be unacceptable behavior—and be willing to use military force if Tehran crosses them. It will also need to reassure its friends and allies in the Middle East that it remains firmly committed to preserving the balance of power in the region.

Containing a nuclear Iran would not be easy. It would require considerable diplomatic skill and political will on the part of the United States. And it could fail. A nuclear Iran may choose to flex its muscles and test U.S. resolve. Even under the best circumstances, the opaque nature of decision-making in Tehran could complicate Washington's efforts to deter it. Thus, it would be far preferable if Iran stopped—or were stopped—before it became a nuclear power. Current efforts to limit Iran's nuclear program must be pursued with vigor. Economic pressure on Tehran must be maintained. Military options to prevent Iran from going nuclear must not be taken off the table.

But these steps may not be enough. If Iran's recalcitrant mullahs cross the nuclear threshold, the challenge for the United States will be to make sure that an abhorrent outcome does not become a catastrophic one. This will require understanding how a nuclear Iran is likely to behave, how its neighbors are likely to respond, and what Washington can do to shape the perceptions and actions of all these players.

MESSIANIC AND PRAGMATIC

IRAN IS a peculiarity: it is a modern-day theocracy that pursues revolutionary ideals while safeguarding its practical interests. After three decades of experimentation, Iran has not outgrown its ideological compunctions. The founder of the Islamic Republic, Ayatollah Ruhollah Khomeini, bequeathed to his successors a clerical cosmology that divides the world between oppressors and oppressed and invests Iran with the mission of redeeming the Middle East for the forces of righteousness. But the political imperative of staying in power has pulled Iran's leaders in a different direction, too: they have had to manage Iran's economy, meet the demands of the country's growing population, and advance Iran's interests in a turbulent region. The clerical rulers have been forced to strike agreements with their rivals and their enemies, occasionally softening the hard edges of their creed. The task of governing has required them to make concessions to often unpalatable realities and has sapped their revolutionary energies. Often, the clash of ideology and pragmatism has put Iran in the paradoxical position of having to secure its objectives within a regional order that it has pledged to undermine.

To satisfy their revolutionary impulses, Iran's leaders have turned anti-Americanism and a strident opposition to Israel into pillars of the state. Tehran supports extremist groups, such as Hamas, Hezbollah, and the Islamist militias opposing U.S. forces in Iraq. The mullahs have sporadically attempted to subvert the U.S.-allied sheikdoms of the Persian Gulf. But the regime has survived because its rulers have recognized the limits of their power and have thus mixed revolutionary agitation with pragmatic adjustment. Although it has denounced the United States as the Great Satan and called for Israel's obliteration, Iran has avoided direct military confrontation with either state. It has vociferously defended the Palestinians, but it has stood by as the Russians have slaughtered Chechens and the Chinese have suppressed Muslim Uighurs. Ideological purity, it seems, has been less important than seeking diplomatic cover from Russia and commercial activity with China. Despite their Islamist compulsions, the mullahs like power too much to be martyrs.

Iran's nuclear program has emerged not just as an important aspect of the country's foreign relations but increasingly as a defining element of its national identity. And the reasons for pursuing the program have changed as it has matured. During the presidencies of Hashemi Rafsanjani and Muhammad Khatami, nuclear weapons were seen as tools of deterrence against the United States and Saddam Hussein's regime, among others. The more conservative current ruling elite, including President Mahmoud Ahmadinejad and the Revolutionary Guards, sees them as a critical means of ensuring Iran's preeminence in the region. A powerful Iran, in other words, requires a robust and extensive nuclear infrastructure. And this may be all the more the case now that Iran is engulfed in the worst domestic turmoil it has known in years: these days, the regime seems to be viewing its quest for nuclear self-sufficiency as a way to revive its own political fortunes.

Going nuclear would empower Iran, but far less than Tehran hopes. Iran's entry into the nuclear club would initially put Tehran in a euphoric mood and likely encourage it to be more aggressive. The mullahs would feel themselves to be in possession of a strategic weapon that would enhance Iran's clout in the region. They might feel less restrained in instigating Shiite uprisings against the Arab sheikdoms in the Persian Gulf. But any efforts to destabilize their Sunni neighbors would meet the same unsuccessful fate as have similar campaigns in the past. Iran's revolutionary message has traditionally appealed to only a narrow segment of Shiites in the Persian Gulf. Sporadic demonstrations in Bahrain and Saudi Arabia have not sought to emulate Iran's revolution; rather, they have been an outlet for Shiites to express their economic and political disenfranchisement.

A nuclear Iran might also be tempted to challenge its neighbors in the Persian Gulf to reduce their oil production and limit the presence of U.S. troops on their territories. However, obtaining nuclear weapons is unlikely to help Iran achieve these aims, because nuclear weapons, by definition, are such a narrow category of arms that they can accomplish only a limited set of objectives. They do offer a deterrent capability: unlike Saddam's Iraq, a nuclear Iran would not be invaded, and its leaders would not be deposed. But regime security and power projection are two very different propositions. It is difficult to imagine Sunni regimes yielding to a resurgent Shiite state, nuclear or not; more likely, the Persian Gulf states would take even more refuge under the U.S. security umbrella. Paradoxically, a weapon that was designed to ensure Iran's regional preeminence could further alienate it from its neighbors and prolong indefinitely the presence of U.S. troops on its periphery. In other words, nuclear empowerment could well thwart Iran's hegemonic ambitions. Like other nuclear aspirants before them, the guardians of the theocracy might discover that nuclear bombs are simply not good for diplomatic leverage or strategic aggrandizement.

Likewise, although the protection of a nuclear Iran might allow Hamas, Hezbollah, and other militant groups in the Middle East to become both more strident in their demands and bolder in their actions, Israel's nuclear arsenal and considerable conventional military power, as well as the United States' support for Israel, would keep those actors in check. To be sure, Tehran will rattle its sabers and pledge its solidarity with Hamas and Hezbollah, but it will not risk a nuclear confrontation with Israel to assist these groups' activities. Hamas and Hezbollah learned from their recent confrontations with Israel that waging war against the Jewish state is a lonely struggle.

The prospect that Iran might transfer a crude nuclear device to its terrorist protégés is another danger, but it, too, is unlikely. Such a move would place Tehran squarely in the cross hairs of the United States and Israel. Despite its messianic pretensions, Iran has observed clear limits when supporting militias and terrorist organizations in the Middle East. Iran has not provided Hezbollah with chemical or biological weapons or Iraqi militias with the means to shoot down U.S. aircraft. Iran's rulers understand that such provocative actions could imperil their rule by inviting retaliation. On the other hand, by coupling strident rhetoric with only limited support in practice, the clerical establishment is able to at once garner popular acclaim for defying the West and oppose the United States and Israel without exposing itself to severe retribution. A nuclear Iran would likely act no differently, at least given the possibility of robust U.S. retaliation. Nor is it likely that Iran would become the new Pakistan, selling nuclear fuel and materials to other states. The prospects of additional sanctions and a military confrontation with the United States are likely to deter Iran from acting impetuously.

A nuclear Iran would undeniably pose new dangers in the Middle East, especially at first, when it would likely be at its most reckless. It might thrash about the Middle East, as it tried to press the presumed advantages of its newfound capability, and it might test the United States' limits. But the mullahs will find it difficult to translate Iran's nuclear status into a tangible political advantage. And if Washington makes clear that rash actions on their part will come at a high cost, they will be far less likely to take any.

THE RIPPLES IN THE REGION

IN ASSESSING the consequences of Iran's nuclearization, it is important to consider not only how Iran is likely to act but also how other states will react to this outcome—and what the United States could do to influence their responses. Iran's nuclearization would not reduce Washington to passively observing events in the region. Washington would retain considerable ability to shape what Iran's neighbors do and do not do.

The nightmare scenario that could be unleashed by Iran's nuclearization is easy to sketch. Israel would go on a hair-trigger alert—ready to launch a nuclear weapon at a moment's notice—putting both countries minutes away from annihilation. Egypt, Saudi Arabia, and Turkey would scramble to join the nuclear club. The Nonproliferation Treaty (NPT) would collapse, unleashing a wave of nuclear proliferation around the globe.

Such a doomsday scenario could pan out. Whether it did would depend greatly on how the United States and others, starting with Israel, responded to Iran's nuclearization. Whether Israeli Prime Minister Benjamin Netanyahu forgoes a preventive strike against Iran's nuclear facilities or opts for launching an attack and it fails, the Israeli government will continue to regard the Iranian regime as an existential threat to Israel that must be countered by any means possible, including the use of nuclear weapons. Given Israel's unique history and Ahmadinejad's contemptible denials of the Holocaust, no Israeli prime minister can afford to think otherwise.

The riskiness of a nuclear standoff between Israel and Iran would vary with the nature and size of Tehran's nuclear arsenal. An Iran with only the capability to build a nuclear weapon would pose a far less immediate threat to Israel than an Iran that possessed an actual weapon. Iran's possession of a bomb would create an inherently unstable situation, in which both parties would have an incentive to strike first: Iran, to avoid losing its arsenal, and Israel, to keep Tehran from using it. The Israeli government's calculations about Iran would depend on its assessment of the United States' willingness and ability to deter Iran. Israel's decision-making would be shaped by a number of factors: the United States' long-standing support for Israel, Israel's doubts about U.S. leadership after Washington's failure to stop Iran from going nuclear, and Washington's response to Iran's nuclearization.

Another danger that would have to be countered would be nuclear proliferation in the Middle East. Iran's regional rivals might try to catch up with it. History suggests, however, that states go nuclear for reasons beyond tit for tat; many hold back even when their enemies get nuclear weapons. China's pursuit of the bomb in the 1960s prompted fears that Japan would follow, but nearly half a century later, Japan remains nonnuclear. Although Israel has more than 200 nuclear weapons, neither its neighbors—not even Egypt, which fought and lost four wars with Israel—nor regional powers, such as Saudi Arabia or Turkey, have followed its lead.

An Iranian nuclear bomb could change these calculations. The U.S. National Intelligence Council concluded in a 2008 report that "Iran's growing nuclear capabilities are already partly responsible for the surge of interest in nuclear energy in the Middle East." And nuclear energy programs can serve as the foundation for drives for nuclear weapons. But it would not be easy for countries in the region to get nuclear weapons. Many lack the infrastructure to develop their own weapons and the missiles needed to deliver them. Egypt and Turkey might blanch at the expense of building a nuclear arsenal. The Pakistanis were willing to "eat grass" for the privilege of joining the nuclear club, as the Pakistani leader Zulfikar Ali Bhutto once famously put it, but not everyone is.

Cost considerations aside, it would take years for nuclear aspirants to develop indigenous nuclear capabilities. They would need to build nuclear reactors, acquire nuclear fuel, master enrichment or reprocessing technologies, and build weapons and the means to deliver them. While they tried, the United States and other states would have ample opportunity to increase the costs of proliferation. Indeed, the economic and security interests of Egypt, Saudi Arabia, and Turkey, unlike those of Iran, are tied to the United States and the broader global economy, and developing nuclear weapons would put those interests at risk. Egypt would jeopardize the $1.5 billion in economic and military aid that it receives from Washington each year; Saudi Arabia, its implicit U.S. security guarantee; and Turkey, its place in NATO. Given their extensive investments in and business ties to the United States and Europe, all three countries would be far more vulnerable than Iran is to any economic sanctions that U.S. law imposed, or could impose, on nuclear proliferators.

States seeking nuclear weapons might try to sidestep these technological and political hurdles by buying, rather than making, the weapons. Saudi Arabia's clandestine acquisition of medium-range ballistic missiles from China in the 1980s suggests that even countries that depend on U.S. security guarantees might be tempted to buy their way into the nuclear club. Although neither the five acknowledged nuclear powers nor India would be likely to sell nuclear weapons to another state, Pakistan and North Korea could be another matter. Both countries have a history of abetting proliferation, and Pakistan has warm ties with its fellow Muslim-majority countries. But selling complete nuclear weapons would come at great political cost. Pakistan might forfeit U.S. foreign assistance and drive the United States into closer cooperation with India, Pakistan's mortal enemy. North Korea would endanger the economic aid it gets from China, which the regime needs to stay in power.

If a buyer did manage to find a seller, it would have to avoid a preventive strike by Israel—which would be likely if the sale became known before the weapon was activated—and then handle the inevitable international political and economic fallout. (In 1988, Saudi Arabia avoided a major rift with Washington over its missile deal with China only by finally agreeing to sign and abide by the NPT.) Furthermore, any country that bought a nuclear weapon would have to worry about whether it would actually work; in global politics, as in everyday life, swindles are possible. Obtaining a nuclear weapon could thus put a country in the worst of all worlds: owning a worthless weapon that is a magnet for an attack.

If Iran's neighbors decided against trying to get nuclear weapons, they could pursue the opposite approach and try to appease Tehran.

The temptation would be greatest for small Persian Gulf states, such as Bahrain and Kuwait, which sit uncomfortably close to Iran and have large Shiite populations. Such a tilt toward Iran would damage U.S. interests in the region. The U.S. Fifth Fleet is based in Bahrain, and U.S. military bases in Bahrain, Kuwait, and the United Arab Emirates are crucial to projecting U.S. power and reassuring U.S. allies in the region. But as long as these governments believe that Washington is committed to their security, appeasement will be unappealing. Pursuing that strategy would mean casting aside U.S. help and betting on the mercy of Tehran. In the absence of a U.S. security guarantee, however, Iran would be free to conduct in those countries the very subversive activities that their governments' appeasement was intended to prevent.

Although Iran's nuclearization would probably not spell the end of efforts to halt proliferation in other parts of the world, it would undeniably deal the nonproliferation regime a setback, by demonstrating that the great powers are unable or unwilling to act collectively to stop proliferators. On the other hand, most states adhere to the NPT because they have compelling national reasons to do so. They may not feel threatened by a nuclear power; they may be covered by the nuclear umbrella of another state; they may lack the financial or technological wherewithal to build a bomb. Iran's success in developing a nuclear weapon would not change these calculations. Nor would it prevent Washington from pushing ahead with its efforts to strengthen the Proliferation Security Initiative (a U.S.-led multinational effort launched by the Bush administration that seeks to stop trafficking in weapons of mass destruction), impose a cutoff on the further production of fissile material, tighten global rules on trade in nuclear materials, and otherwise make it more difficult for nuclear technologies to spread.

Iran's acquisition of a nuclear bomb could have disastrous consequences in the Middle East. But Washington would have considerable opportunities to influence, and constrain, how Iran's neighbors reacted to its new status. It would matter whether Washington reassured Israel or fueled its fears. It would matter whether Washington confronted regional proliferation efforts or turned a blind eye, as it did with Pakistan in the 1980s. It would matter whether Washington pushed ahead with efforts to strengthen the NPT regime or threw in the towel. To keep the nightmare scenario at bay, the United States will need to think carefully about how to maximize its leverage in the region.

I SAY NO, NO, NO

TEHRAN IS an adversary that speaks in ideological terms, wants to become a dominant regional power, and is capable of acting recklessly. But it is also an adversary that recognizes its limitations, wants to preserve its hold on power, and operates among wary neighbors. Its acquiring a nuclear bomb, or the capacity to make a nuclear bomb, need not remake the Middle East—at least not if the United States acts confidently and wisely to exploit Iran's weaknesses.

Any strategy to contain Iran must begin with the recognition that this effort will have to be different from that to contain the Soviet Union. Iran poses a different threat. During the early years of the Cold War, U.S. policymakers tried to protect like-minded countries against a Soviet invasion that would have imposed communist rule, or against widespread economic dislocation, which could have produced a communist takeover from within. Their strategy was to turn to the NATO alliance and launch the Marshall Plan. The United States' containment strategy toward Iran must reflect different realities today. Iran does not seek to invade its neighbors, and its ideological appeal does not rest on promises of economic justice. It seeks to establish itself as the dominant power in the region while preserving political control at home.

Deterrence would by necessity be the cornerstone of a U.S. strategy to contain a nuclear Iran. Success is by no means guaranteed. Deterrence can fail: it nearly did during the Cuban missile crisis, in 1962, and at several other critical junctures of the Cold

War. Iran's revisionist aims and paranoia about U.S. power may appear to make the country uniquely difficult to deter. But that conclusion conveniently—and mistakenly—recasts the history of U.S. confrontations with emerging nuclear powers in a gentler light than is deserved. At the start of the Cold War, U.S. officials hardly saw the Soviet Union as a status quo power. In the 1960s, China looked like the ultimate rogue regime: it had intervened in Korea and gone to war with India, and it repressed its own people. Mao boasted that although nuclear war might kill half the world's population, it would also mean that "imperialism would be razed to the ground and the whole world would become socialist."

Today, the challenge for U.S. policymakers devising a deterrence strategy toward Iran will be to unambiguously identify what behavior they seek to deter—and what they are willing to do about it. When Washington publicly presents its policy on how to contain a nuclear Iran, it should be explicit: no initiation of conventional warfare against other countries; no use or transfer of nuclear weapons, materials, or technologies; and no stepped-up support for terrorist or subversive activities. It should also make clear that the price of Iran's violating these three prohibitions could be U.S. military retaliation by any and all means necessary, up to and including nuclear weapons.

The pledge to deter a conventional attack would be the easiest of the three prohibitions to enforce. Iran's ability to project sustained military power outside its borders is limited. And it is unlikely to grow substantially anytime soon: even more arms embargoes would likely be imposed on Iran if it crossed the nuclear threshold. At their current level, U.S. troops in the region are more than sufficient to deter Iran from undertaking incursions into Iraq or amphibious operations across the Persian Gulf—or to stop them if they occurred.

Deterring Iran from using or threatening to use nuclear weapons would present a different set of challenges. So long as Iran lacks the ability to strike the United States with a nuclear-tipped missile, the United States can credibly threaten to retaliate militarily if Iran uses or threatens to use a nuclear bomb against anyone. But that could change if Iran developed long-range missiles. Tehran might also try to deter the United States by threatening to attack Europe, which would raise well-known concerns about the viability of so-called extended deterrence, the ability of one state to deter an attack on another. These possibilities highlight the importance of developing robust, multilayered ballistic missile defenses. The Obama administration's decision to reorient U.S. missile defenses in Europe to protect against shorter-range missiles while continuing to develop defenses against longer-range missiles is just the right approach.

A tougher challenge would be to ensure stable deterrence between Iran and Israel. With regard to this issue, too, the Iranian nuclear program's ultimate degree of development would be pivotal: an Iran armed with nuclear weapons would present a significantly more dangerous threat than one that merely had the capacity to build them. It is thus essential that Washington continue to apply diplomatic and economic pressure to keep Tehran, should it manage to complete the nuclear fuel cycle, from taking the final step. The United States should also publicly pledge to retaliate by any means it chooses if Iran uses nuclear weapons against Israel; this would in effect supplement whatever second-strike capability Israel has. If the Israelis need a formal commitment to be more reassured, this pledge could be made in an executive agreement or a treaty. As a tangible expression of its commitment, Washington should also be prepared to deploy U.S. troops on Israeli soil as a tripwire, which would show that the United States would be inextricably bound to Israel in the event of any Iranian attack.

Washington should also inform Tehran that it would strike preemptively, with whatever means it deemed necessary, if Iran ever placed its nuclear forces on alert. And it should bring both Israel and Israel's Arab neighbors fully under its missile defense umbrella. The more aggressive Iran is, the more inclined its neighbors will be to work with Washington to construct missile defenses on their territories.

Deterring Iran from transferring nuclear weapons, materials, and technologies to state and nonstate actors would require another set of measures. For the most part, Iran has reasons not to pursue such perilous activities, but it could be tempted to exploit the difficulty of tracking the clandestine trade in nuclear materials. The United States and its allies would need to act decisively to prevent Tehran from seeking to profit in the international nuclear bazaar, for example, through the Proliferation Security Initiative and through UN resolutions that imposed additional sanctions on Iran and its potential business partners. To impress on Iran's ruling mullahs that it is singularly important for them to control whatever nuclear arsenal they may develop or obtain, Washington should hold Tehran responsible for any nuclear transfer, whether authorized or not; Tehran cannot be allowed to escape punishment or retaliation by pleading loss of control. Increased investments in monitoring and spying on Iran would be critical. The United States must improve its ability to track nuclear weapons, materials, and debris and prove and publicize whether they came from Iran (or any other country, for that matter). Such nuclear forensics is crucial to determining who is responsible for nuclear transfers and would be crucial to building support for any U.S. retaliation against Iran, if it were the culprit.

Deterring Iranian support for terrorist and subversive groups—the third redline prohibition that the United States should impose— would be difficult. Such activities take place secretly, making it hard to establish precisely who is complicit. That complication places a premium on improving the ability of the U.S. intelligence community, acting alone and in concert with its counterparts abroad, to track Iran's clandestine activities.

WHATS AND WHAT NOTS

IN ADDITION to holding Iran accountable for violating any of the three noes, the United States' containment strategy should seek to influence and, where necessary, constrain Iran's friends in the Middle East. An energetic diplomacy that softened the disagreements between Israel and its neighbors would undermine Iran's efforts to exploit anger in the region. A concerted push, diplomatic and economic, to improve the lives of the Palestinians would limit Iran's appeal among them. Drawing Syria into a comprehensive Israeli-Palestinian peace process could not only attenuate Tehran's links with Damascus but also stem Iran's ability to supply weapons to Hezbollah. Washington should seek to further limit Iran's strategic reach by strengthening the institutional and military capabilities of Afghanistan and Iraq. It should reassure the Persian Gulf states that it is committed to preserving the existing balance of power, which would require expanding trade agreements, enhancing their security and intelligence apparatuses, and developing a more integrated approach to defense planning in the region. At the same time, the United States will need to dissuade these governments from further suppressing their Shiite minorities, a practice that inadvertently aids Tehran. And it should work assiduously to prevent more countries in the Middle East from going nuclear; the United States cannot look the other way again, as it did with Pakistan during the 1980s.

Tone and conviction will matter. Washington must keep in mind that Iran's entry into the nuclear club would be read by Israel and Arab states as a failure of the United States' political will and a demonstration of the limits of U.S. power. Washington cannot afford to compound its credibility problem by hesitating or vacillating. An indecisive U.S. response would undermine the efforts both to deter Iran and to reassure U.S. friends and allies in the region.

Washington should also push other major powers to contain the Iranian threat. The five permanent members of the UN Security Council have sponsored numerous resolutions demanding that Iran cease its nuclear activities and cooperate with the International Atomic Energy Agency. They should have a vested interest in punishing Iran, an original signatory to the NPT, if it reneges on its decades-old pledge to remain a nonnuclear power. Doing nothing would substantially undermine the UN Security Council's authority and with it their status as permanent members of the council. Europe should be pressed to commit troops and naval vessels to preserve the free flow of traffic through the Persian Gulf. Russia should cease its nuclear cooperation with and its conventional arms sales to Iran. China should be pressed to curtail its investment in Iran's energy sector, which does so much to fuel Iran's belligerence. The United States would have to do much of the heavy lifting in containing a nuclear Iran, but any concerted containment strategy must have not just regional support but also an international complexion.

Just as important as what Washington should do to contain Iran is what it should not do. If Iran gets a nuclear bomb, the United States might be tempted to respond by substantially expanding the presence of U.S. troops in the Middle East. But this would not appreciably increase Washington's ability to deter Iran from launching a nuclear or conventional attack; there are already enough U.S. forces in the region for that. It could, however, play into the hands of Tehran's proxies by inflaming anti-American sentiment and fanning civil unrest in the Persian Gulf.

Washington might also be tempted to seek to further undermine Iran's economy by imposing broad-based economic sanctions, an idea that enjoys considerable support on Capitol Hill. But such measures would wind up punishing only Iran's disenfranchised citizenry (which is why Iranian opposition leaders have strenuously opposed them). The wiser course of action would be to strengthen and better monitor existing export controls, in order to make certain that Iran's nuclear and defense industries do not have access to dual-use technologies, and to reinforce targeted sanctions against the Iranian leadership and the business enterprises controlled by the Revolutionary Guards. Washington should push, both inside and outside the UN, for travel bans on Iranian leaders and measures denying

Iran access to capital markets, for example. It should also find ways to penalize foreign businesses that invest in Iran's dilapidated oil industry. Smart sanctions of this kind would punish Iran's leaders but spare ordinary Iranians, who have no say over the regime's actions.

The United States should refrain from greatly expanding the range of weaponry it sells to the Persian Gulf states, which see the United States as a military guarantor and their chief arms supplier. To some extent, increasing arms sales will be necessary: the Arab governments of the region would regard such sales as a tangible sign of the strength of Washington's commitment to their defense, and if Washington holds back, these governments will look for weapons elsewhere. On the other hand, throwing the doors of the armory wide open would do little to secure the buyers and might even increase instability in the region. A smart U.S. arms sales policy would focus on offering weapons systems that are designed to deter or help counter an Iranian attack, such as missile defense systems and command-and-control systems, which would provide advance notice of Iranian actions.

Finally, Washington should resist any urge to sign mutual security treaties with Arab countries in the Middle East. (Israel, whose relations with Iran are fundamentally different from those of every other power in the region, is a special case.) Such efforts would do little to enhance deterrence and could do a lot to undermine it. Many members of the U.S. Senate, which would have to vote on any alliance treaty, would question whether the United States should further tie itself to authoritarian regimes that many Americans find odious. The spectacle of that debate would exacerbate doubts in the Middle East about the depth of the United States' commitment. Efforts to construct formal alliances might also lead Iran to believe that any country left out of these agreements is fair game for intimidation or attack. Washington should be mindful not to invite a replay of North Korea's calculation in 1950 that South Korea lay outside the U.S. defense perimeter.

Instead, the U.S. government should encourage the formation of a regional alliance network that would marshal Arab states into a more cohesive defense grouping. The network could be organized along the lines of the Middle East Treaty Organization (then the Central Treaty Organization), a security arrangement among Iran, Pakistan, Turkey, the United Kingdom, and, for a time, Iraq (with the United States participating in the organization's military and security committees) that existed from 1955 to 1979. An alliance of this kind would secure all the benefits of a regionwide commitment to deterrence without exposing the United States and its allies to the complexities of formal bilateral or multilateral security treaties.

DANGEROUS TIMES

IRAN'S NUCLEARIZATION would make the Middle East a more dangerous place: it would heighten tensions, reduce the margin for error, and raise the prospect of mass catastrophe. The international community should not let up on its efforts to stop Iran's progress. But given the mullahs' seeming indifference to the benefits of engagement, U.S. policymakers must consider now what to do if Iran does get the bomb.

Containment would be neither a perfect nor a foolproof policy. The task of foiling Iran's support for Hamas and Hezbollah would be difficult, as would countering Iran's support for terrorist and subversive groups in the region. The need to gain favor with Arab dictatorships would likely tempt Washington to shelve its calls for domestic political reforms in those countries—even though such reforms could diminish Iran's ability to meddle there by improving the lot of local minority Shiites who might otherwise be susceptible to Tehran's influence. Maintaining great-power support for pressure on Iran could require overlooking objectionable Chinese and Russian behavior on other matters. Containment would not be a substitute for the use of force. To the contrary, its very success would depend on the willingness of the United States to use force against Iran or threaten to do so should Tehran cross Washington's redlines. Applying pressure without a commitment to punishing infractions is a recipe for failure—and for a more violent and dangerous Middle East.

Containment could buy Washington time to persuade the Iranian ruling class that the revisionist game it has been playing is simply not worth the candle. Thus, even as Washington pushes to counter Iran, it should be open to the possibility that Tehran's calculations might change. To press Tehran in the right direction, Washington should signal that it seeks to create an order in the Middle East that is peaceful and self-sustaining. The United States will remain part of the region's security architecture for the foreseeable future, but it need not maintain an antagonistic posture toward Iran. An Islamic Republic that abandoned its nuclear ambitions, accepted prevailing international norms, and respected the sovereignty of its neighbors would discover that the United States is willing to work with, rather than against, Iran's legitimate national aspirations.🌐

Obama's Counterproductive New Iran Sanctions

How Washington is Sliding Toward Regime Change

Suzanne Maloney

ForeignAffairs.com, January 5, 2012

TENSIONS BETWEEN the United States and Iran have spiked once again. Last week, responding to planned U.S. sanctions against Iran's central bank, Tehran threatened to close the Strait of Hormuz, the shipping gateway for one-fifth of the world's oil. U.S. President Barack Obama, pressed by Congress' near-universal support for tough new measures to force Iran to abandon its nuclear ambitions, decided to go ahead with the sanctions and signed them into law on Saturday. Fully enforced, they would slash one of Iran's foremost state revenue streams and virtually excise one of the world's leading oil exporters from the marketplace.

The chain of events fueled concerns that Washington might be stumbling into a third war in the Middle East. But a more fundamental problem underlies these developments. The Obama administration's new sanctions signal the demise of the paradigm that had guided U.S. Iran policymaking since the 1979 revolution: the combination of pressure and persuasion. Moreover, the decision to outlaw contact with Iran's central bank puts the United States'

SUZANNE MALONEY is a Senior Fellow at the Saban Center for Middle East Policy at the Brookings Institution.

tactics and its long-standing objective—a negotiated end to Iran's nuclear ambitions—at odds. Indeed, the United States cannot hope to bargain with a country whose economy it is trying to disrupt and destroy. As severe sanctions devastate Iran, Tehran will surely be encouraged to double down on its quest for the ultimate deterrent. So, the White House's embrace of open-ended pressure means that it has backed itself into a policy of regime change, something Washington has little ability to influence.

For the moment, at least, the central bank sanctions remain a work in progress. The text of the law provides the executive branch with reasonable flexibility, including a national security waiver. It also appears to condition enforcement on world oil supply considerations and offers foreign governments a six-month amnesty period, during which they may figure out where else to buy crude, or, presumably, develop workarounds to continue buying from Tehran. Obama hedged, too, by appending a signing statement to the bill, asserting his right to disregard any measures that impinge on his authority to set U.S. foreign policy. To be sure, perfect enforcement of the sanctions regime would drive up the price of oil. And election-year concerns about the economy could ultimately trump Obama's determination to penalize Iran. Still, Congress may have other ideas.

Senior U.S. officials are bullish on the prospective impact of sanctioning Tehran's central bank. Allies such as Japan and South Korea, which together account for approximately one-third of Iran's crude exports, will follow Washington's lead. U.S. officials also point to Tehran's announcement that it is once again ready to meet with the P5 plus 1 (the multilateral group that has spearheaded Iranian nuclear talks, albeit with little success) as evidence that increasing pressure is focusing the minds of Iranian leaders.

Such optimism, however, is premature. Tehran has a penchant for signaling just enough interest in negotiations to retain a measure of goodwill among some segments of the international community—particularly countries in Asia that are increasingly vital for Iran's economic stability. Tehran might calculate that a show of receptivity could undermine the fragile consensus between the hawkish Americans and the Europeans, who are moving forward with their own ban on Iranian crude, and their more sanctions-averse partners in Moscow and Beijing. There is also, of course, Iran's well-honed capacity for sanctions-busting and evasion, which will blunt the impact of these new sanctions.

Lest Washington forgets, the Islamic Republic has endured more draconian economic pressures in the past. Despite its phenomenal petroleum resources, rarely in its 32-year history has the Islamic Republic been flush. During the height of its war with Iraq, Iran's annual oil revenues fell under $6 billion—less than ten percent of its 2010 take. Skyrocketing income from oil sales over the last decade has been a welcome anomaly for Iran's revolutionaries, but it is hardly certain that constricting that spigot will doom the regime, much less force it to capitulate on the nuclear issue. Tehran remains confident in its ability to adopt austerity as needed. In fact, blaming an international bogeyman will offer convenient cover for the regime's own economic mismanagement.

The Obama administration has argued that "pressure works," pointing to past reversals by the Islamic Republic, including the grudging and belated acceptance of a cease-fire to end its eight-year war with Iraq. Yet this formula disregards two critical points: first, Tehran has been under tremendous pressure to change its security policy throughout its entire post-revolutionary history, yet that policy has proved remarkably durable. Second, Iran's major concessions have come not simply as a product of pressure but because of the declining utility of the original objective. In this instance, however, the tables are turned. The more Washington corners Tehran, the higher the value of a nuclear deterrent becomes in the eyes of the leadership.

Although this suggests more friction ahead, it does not mean that a military clash is absolutely on the horizon. Neither side wants war: not Washington, which has worked assiduously to meet the president's timetable for winding down the two other military engagements in the broader Middle East, and not Tehran, which prefers the more familiar (and lower-risk) options availed through proxies and terrorist activities. A prolonged low-intensity struggle—with plenty of blustery rhetoric and diplomatic hard-ball—is now the new normal.

What needs to be addressed is the disturbing reality that the Obama administration's approach offers no viable endgame for dealing with Iran's current leadership. The impression that the sanctions are permanent—indeed, the new law does not specify any conditions that Tehran might satisfy in order to lift the siege on its central bank—conforms to Iranian hard-liners' darkest delusions about Washington's intentions. By embracing maximalist measures, the White House has come full circle, abandoning, along the way, its earlier optimistic efforts at engagement. In doing so, it has implicitly relinquished the prospect of negotiating with the Islamic regime: given the ayatollahs' innate mistrust of the West, they cannot be nudged into a constructive negotiating process by measures that exacerbate their vulnerability.

American policy is now effectively predicated on achieving political change in Tehran. Such an outcome will likely prove even more elusive than productive talks with the revolutionary regime—something the United States has sought for 33 years.❧

Tehran Takedown

How to Spark an Iranian Revolution

Michael Ledeen

ForeignAffairs.com, July 31, 2012

THE NUCLEAR question is at the center of most countries' Iran policies. China, France, Germany, Russia, the United Kingdom, and the United States have all engaged in negotiations to convince Tehran to give up its presumed quest for the bomb. Now, with talks sputtering, Western powers have implemented increasingly tough sanctions, including the European Union's recent embargo on Iranian oil, in the hope of compelling the regime to reverse course.

Yet history suggests, and even many sanctions advocates agree, that sanctions will not compel Iran's leaders to scrap their nuclear program. In fact, from Fidel Castro's Cuba to Saddam Hussein's Iraq, hostile countries have rarely changed policy in response to Western embargoes. Some sanctions advocates counter that sanctions did work to get Chile to abandon communism, South Africa to end apartheid, and Libya to give up its nuclear program. But the Chilean and South African governments were not hostile—they were pro-Western, and thus more amenable to the West's demands. And Libya's Muammar al-Qaddafi ended his nuclear pursuit only after the

---

MICHAEL LEDEEN is Freedom Scholar at the Foundation for Defense of Democracies. His blog, *Faster, Please*, is at PJ Media.

2003 U.S. invasion of Iraq, fearing that he would suffer the same fate as Saddam Hussein.

Iran, which is clearly hostile and which watched what just happened to a disarmed Libya, will not back down. Some therefore see sanctions as only a prelude to military action—by Israel, the United States, or both. In other words, current Iran strategy boils down to an eventual choice between appeasement and attack. Neither outcome is attractive. However, if the United States and its allies broadened their perspective and paid attention not merely to Iran's nuclear program but also to the Islamic Republic's larger assault on the West, they would see that a third and better option exists: supporting a democratic revolution in Iran.

Obsession with the nuclear question has obscured the fact that, since the 1979 Islamic Revolution, Iran has waged a low-level war on the United States. That war began in earnest in 1983, when, evidence suggests, Iranian-backed operatives bombed the U.S. Marine barracks in Beirut. Such violence continued throughout the 1980s, as Hezbollah, a terrorist organization created by Iran, kidnapped and murdered Americans in Lebanon. In addition to supporting Hezbollah, Iran started funding other terrorist groups, such as Hamas, Islamic Jihad, and the Popular Front for the Liberation of Palestine. In the last decade, Iranian agents have attacked U.S. troops in Afghanistan and Iraq. Late last year, the Obama administration revealed that Iranian agents had attempted to assassinate the Saudi Arabian ambassador to the United States and to blow up the Saudi and Israeli embassies in Washington, D.C.

In short, the nuclear program is not the central issue in Iran policymaking—defending the United States and its allies from Iranian terrorists and their proxies is. To meet that goal, Washington must replace the Islamic Republic's regime. The theocrats in Tehran call the United States "the great Satan," and waging war against it is one of the Iranian leadership's core missions. The Ayatollah Khomeini proclaimed that as his goal very soon after the shah was overthrown in 1979. Calls of "Death to America" have been a constant refrain ever since. Regime change cannot be achieved by sanctions and diplomacy alone. And, although war might bring down the regime, it is neither necessary nor desirable. Supporting a domestic revolution is a wiser strategy.

The Iranian regime is not only at war with the United States and its allies; it is also at war with its own people. It represses Iranian citizens, restricting their civil liberties and imprisoning, torturing, and killing political opponents. Popular discontent boiled over into open protest after a rigged election in June 2009, as what came to be known as the Green Movement launched an open challenge to the political status quo. The regime brutally suppressed the protests and is keeping the movement's two leaders, presidential candidates Mir Hossein Mousavi and Mehdi Karroubi, along with Mousavi's wife, under house arrest.

Conventional wisdom describes the Green Movement as a spent force, citing the lack of mass demonstrations over the past year and half. Iranian authorities regularly restrict and censor the Internet and intercept and block cell phone and satellite communications, and they have increased deployments of security forces in cities across the country. In such an atmosphere, skeptics argue, there can be little opposition to speak of, let alone one with the leadership and mass support to challenge the regime.

But this was also the conventional wisdom back in early 2009, and it is as wrong now as it was then. The West was caught unawares by the explosion of popular rage after Mousavi's election was stolen, and it failed to support the opposition. The regime paid no price for its crackdown.

In fact, despite the government lockdown, dissenters today have continued to strike out against the regime through acts such as the sabotage of oil and natural gas pipelines. The disruption of the natural gas line between Iran and Turkey in late June, which was reported by the state-run *Press TV*, is only the latest of many such attacks. Last March, opposition activists privately claimed responsibility for attacks on two Revolutionary Guards Corps installations. One was Zarin Dasht, where missile fuel and warheads are manufactured. The other was Natanz, a major uranium enrichment center. The explosion took place deep underground, leading to a shutdown of the entire complex.

Meanwhile, although the Green Movement's leaders are still under house arrest, they continue to issue statements to their supporters. And according to a recent online government poll, the population is fed up. Nearly two-thirds of respondents said that they favored giving up the nuclear program in exchange for an end to sanctions. The poll was quickly yanked off the Web site.

For their part, Iranian authorities are worried. In January, Ali Saeedi, Khamenei's representative to the Islamic Revolutionary Guards Corps, admitted that the regime continues to fear the strength of the Green Movement. Regime leaders are at pains to reassure the public that Mousavi and Karroubi are being well treated. If Iranian Supreme Leader Ayatollah Ali Khamenei wanted to demonstrate the weakness of the opposition, he would have subjected both to the same harsh treatment that has been meted out to many of their followers. But as Saeedi told Fars, the Iranian state news agency, Mousavi and Karroubi have "supporters and followers," as well as "a few [clerics] who continue to back elements within the sedition"—the term used by the regime to refer to the Green Movement.

The regime's anxiety about the Green Movement also led it to delay all elections in the country for three years. And when it finally held parliamentary elections this past May, it banned scores of candidates from running and deployed thousands of security forces at polling stations to prevent protests. Their fear might also be the reason that Khamenei avoided speaking at the Revolutionary Guards Day festivities in late June, the first time he had done so in over two decades. Similarly, the regime has reduced the number of anti-American protests it stages, perhaps worrying that the reformers would hijack them. When two popular (and apolitical) Iranian artists died this summer—the actor Iraj Ghaderi and the musician Hassan Kassai—their funerals were held without fanfare and in the middle of the night. The regime is clearly doing all it can to keep Iranians from gathering in the streets.

By themselves, the strength of the opposition and the regime's fears do not justify Western intervention. After all, several Middle Eastern dictators have fallen of late, only to be replaced by actors more hostile to U.S. interests. And some experts contend that the same could happen in Iran. Mousavi served as prime minister of Iran from 1981 to 1989 and played a key role in the creation of the Islamic Republic. Many, including U.S. President Barack Obama, have raised the possibility that his accession might not change much. So, before jumping into the fray on behalf of the opposition, the United States and its allies must ask whether the Green Movement would end Iran's support for terrorism against the United States and its allies, stop oppressing its own people, and terminate the country's nuclear weapons program.

Although it is dangerous for opposition leaders to be totally explicit about all such matters, their answers are encouraging. During the 2009 electoral campaign, and on several subsequent occasions, Mousavi promised to end Iranian backing for terrorist organizations—a promise that resonates with large numbers of Iranian citizens. In February 2011, demonstrators carried banners decrying the regime's support for foreign terrorist groups, with slogans such as "Don't talk to us about the Palestinians, talk about us."

The Green Movement has also pledged to dismantle many oppressive practices of the Islamic Republic. Although the group's leaders claim that they want to restore the values of the 1979 revolution, during the 2009 presidential election, Mousavi's wife, Zahra Rahnavard, campaigned alongside him and declared her support of women who dispense with wearing the veil. It was a stark act of defiance against a deeply misogynistic regime. Mousavi, meanwhile, has promised tolerance of religious dissenters, the release of all political prisoners, and greater separation of church and state. As the Green leaders wrote to the Obama administration in November 2009, "religion, by the will of the Iranian people of today, has to be separated from the state in order to guarantee unity of Iran."

Even from house arrest, Mousavi has continued to send signals that he would overturn the policies of the current regime. In the past year, he urged Iranians to read two books: *News of a Kidnapping*, by Gabriel Garcia Marquez, and *The Right to Heresy*, by Stefan Zweig. The first volume, which deals with a wave of kidnappings in Colombia by drug gangs, inspired a popular Iranian Facebook page called "News of a Kidnapping, the status of a president in captivity." The second book addresses a revolt against John Calvin by the sixteenth century cleric Sebastian Castellio, after the torture and execution of the heretic Michael Servetus. It is at once a call for religious toleration and an essay on those thinkers who were crushed during their lifetime, only to emerge triumphant in death. By turning to these texts, Mousavi issued a direct challenge to Khamenei and oriented his movement with Western values.

It is hard to pinpoint the nuclear intentions of the Green Movement's leaders, but there is reason for guarded optimism; they have repeatedly condemned the regime's "adventurism" in foreign affairs, and would certainly seek better relations with the West. As Iranian crude oil production drops, a democratic Iran might opt for nuclear energy, but it seems unlikely that such a government would continue the secret weapons program. And the West, including Israel, would have far less to fear from a free Iran, whatever weapons it might possess, than it does from the current regime.

Given the potential for a successful democratic revolution in Iran—and the potential for a democratic government to end

Iran's war against us—the question is how the United States and its allies can best support the Green Movement.

Although an Iranian revolution may seem unlikely to the casual observer, the Iranian people can be said to have revolution in their DNA, having carried out three revolutions in the twentieth century. Many skeptics argue that any Western aid to the Green Movement would delegitimize it in such a nationalist country. Yet, during the mass demonstrations in 2009 and 2010, protesters waved signs and banners saying "Obama, where are you?" Moreover, in a carefully unsigned letter to the White House in late 2009, Green Movement leaders responded to an administration query by saying that "it is up to the countries of the free world to make up their mind. Will they . . . push every decision to the future until it is too late, or will they reward the brave people of Iran and simultaneously advance Western interests and world peace?"

Even so, the West snubbed the uprising, insisting that the Iranian opposition did not want outside help. As far as I know, there is no evidence to suggest that an attempt has been made since then to speak directly with the Green Movement inside the country. (Mousavi has said several times that the Green Movement does not have spokespeople or representatives outside Iran.) Unable or unwilling to engage with the opposition, the West has devoted its energy to the nuclear question alone, pursuing a policy that will produce war or diplomatic and strategic failure.

That is why the time has come for the United States and other Western nations to actively support Iran's democratic dissidents. The same methods that took down the Soviet regime should work: call for the end of the regime, broadcast unbiased news about Iran to the Iranian people, demand the release of political prisoners (naming them whenever possible), help those prisoners communicate with one another, enlist international trade unions to build a strike fund for Iranian workers, and perhaps find ways to provide other kinds of economic and technological support. Meanwhile, the West should continue nuclear negotiations and stick to the sanctions regime, which shows the Iranian people resistance to their oppressive leaders.

Iran's democratic revolutionaries themselves must decide what kind of Western help they most need, and how to use it. But they will be greatly encouraged to see the United States and its allies behind them. There are many good reasons to believe that this strategy can succeed. Not least, the Iranian people have already demonstrated their willingness to confront the regime; the regime's behavior shows its fear of the people. The missing link is a Western decision to embrace and support democratic revolution in Iran—the country that, after all, initiated the challenge to the region's tyrants three summers ago.⊛

Other Voices

Sanctions Won't End Iran's Nuclear Program

Letter From Tehran

Kayhan Barzegar

ForeignAffairs.com, *February 9, 2012*

WITH THE recent European ban on importing Iranian oil, the West has ratcheted up its pressure on Tehran another notch. The United States argues that the goal is to bring Iran back to the negotiating table to ensure that it doesn't weaponize its nuclear program. From Iran's perspective, however, the West's purpose is not to talk but to stop Iran's enrichment of uranium altogether.

Indeed, at the same time that it calls for talks, the West—and especially the United States—has continued to implement new sanctions. Many Iranians also believe that the United States is waging a covert war against their country and see the Stuxnet computer worm (which seemed to target industrial equipment in Iran's nuclear facilities) and recent assassinations of Iranian scientists as part of it. Washington's allegations in October 2011 that Tehran was involved in a plot against the Saudi ambassador to the United States—and its subsequent violation of Iran's airspace with an unmanned drone—have only reinforced Iranian unease.

KAYHAN BARZEGAR is Director of the Institute for Middle East Strategic Studies and Chair of the Department of Political Science and International Relations at the Science and Research Branch of the Islamic Azad University in Tehran.

That ill feeling is an impediment to any serious talks between Iran and the West. Deteriorating U.S.-Iranian relations will weaken the consensus among Iranian decision-makers to go through with negotiations. They see talks as a part of a broader effort to make progress on all issues of common interest, including regional peace and security. But Iran's ability to enrich uranium at home remains the core matter. If the ruling elite suspect that Iran will be forced to give up uranium enrichment for civilian purposes, political leaders will simply reject further talks with the P5 plus 1, made up of the permanent members of the UN Security Council and Germany. And the EU's signing on to oil sanctions last month has made rejection even more likely. Until now, the EU had been seen as something of a mediator, but now it seems to be pitted firmly against Iran.

The West's behavior will also weaken support for the nuclear talks among the Iranian public. The harsher and broader sanctions become, the more impact they have on people's daily lives. Just after the EU announced its ban (which would go into effect in July of 2012), the Iranian parliament drafted legislation preemptively banning oil exports to Europe. Since then, students from different universities have banded together to lobby parliament to expedite the new law's approval. Further outrage would lead to increased tensions, making it even more difficult for the government to enter into any new talks.

For its part, the West often turns a blind eye to the fact that, since Iran has already developed an indigenous enrichment capability, it is irreversibly a nuclear power—even if it were to hypothetically put an end to enriching uranium in the short term. After all, Iran will always retain nuclear know-how and capability. It will always be a nuclear power. Any meaningful negotiation should thus start from that fact.

Even without weaponization, moreover, the country values its nuclear capability as a strategic deterrent. At any point, the United States' current rhetoric on Iran could escalate into a war. Iran is unlikely to agree to a zero-enrichment policy because, in doing so, it would give up its most valuable bargaining chip—the one that brings the West to the table in the first place. The West surely understands this, and knows that raising the issue is a nonstarter.

The West's behavior is also counterproductive to talks because sanctions degrade Iran's political equality during nuclear negotiations. When in a weakened position, Iranians would likely not embark on meaningful negotiations. The fear of losing would unquestionably lead many in Tehran to refuse to enter talks to begin with.

That is why every previous attempt by the West to step up pressure on Iran was met with Iranian attempts to put the relationship back on equal footing. For example, the Security Council's many resolutions against the nuclear program in the past six years led Iran to build approximately 8,000 more centrifuges, increase the degree of enrichment by 20 percent, establish a new nuclear site, and move many enrichment activities to a site at Fordo, which is far more hardened than other facilities against attack. Iran has also recently expressed its determination to use 20 percent indigenous enriched fuel in the Tehran Research Reactor in the near future.

Iran's threat last month to shut down the Strait of Hormuz is another case in point. Many in the West have said that Tehran will not make good on those words because it cannot block its own oil exports. That is true, in part, but if sanctions put the country in an increasingly perilous economic situation, Iran may have no choice but to close the Strait and wreak havoc on the rest of the world economy in the hope of having sanctions lifted.

For now, however, things are not likely to get that bad. The latest EU sanctions will decrease Iran's oil exports by only 18 percent. If Asian nations also embrace the sanctions, disrupting Iran's oil exports to China, India, and Japan, however, Tehran would respond more forcefully. That is unlikely; there are limits to China and Russia's willingness to go along with more sanctions. For one, Russian-U.S. relations have chilled recently over

Washington's installation of a missile defense shield on Turkish soil. Their differing approaches to the Arab Spring did not help matters. And China, having benefited from importing energy from Iran and exporting goods to it, is reluctant to support the United States' policies. Both countries will thus likely veto a resolution in the Security Council for more sanctions or a military action against Iran.

Moreover, emerging powers such as India and Turkey are aware that they could not easily find a substitute for Iran's oil. They know that any disruption in the world oil market would also jeopardize their economic security. Accordingly, they have gone a step further than China and Russia and have explicitly declared their unwillingness to stop energy cooperation with Iran.

Some Arab states in the Middle East, such as Saudi Arabia, might want to see Iran struggling under stepped-up sanctions, but even they are absolutely cognizant of the fact that any major disruption in the oil market could lead to deepening tensions, instability, or even war in the region. In the wake of the Arab Spring, the rulers of those countries are wary of further regional disruption, so they might change their stance on the embargo to avoid a major conflict in their backyards. At any critical juncture, Iran is likely to take measures to disrupt the hostile Arab states' oil shipping lines, as it did during the "tanker war" in the 1980s.

Iran's nuclear program will not live or die because of economic sanctions. Such pressures simply will not change the country's nuclear policy. The idea that they could is based on the faulty belief that multilateral action and the threat of war could bring Tehran back to the negotiating table, and, ultimately, push it to surrender all uranium enrichment programs. Not only will sanctions do no such thing, they will unite all of Iran's political factions under a pro-nuclear banner, making talks impossible.

So, although the West can escalate pressure and sanctions, Iran can increase its nuclear activities at any time. Iran and the West both consider themselves on the threshold of a victory in the marathon race against each other. Their misevaluations of each other's determination have trapped them in an increasing cycle of distrust, tension, and military buildup. More than nuclear programs, these misconceptions should concern the international community. Waging war would be catastrophic for both sides—and for the rest of the world.

Therefore, Iran and the West should immediately seek a way to smooth over this rough patch. The problem can be addressed through interaction and diplomacy. Balancing the legitimate right of Iran to use peaceful nuclear energy under the NPT and the prohibition of its diversion towards weaponization is the most important matter. The main issue for Iran is trusting the West not to demand an end to its native nuclear program. By taking that off the table, the West could show its seriousness about the nuclear talks.❷

How to Engage Iran

What Went Wrong Last Time—And How to Fix It

Hossein Mousavian

ForeignAffairs.com, February 9, 2012

SINCE THE 1979 Islamic Revolution, two major schools of thought have influenced Iran's foreign policy toward the United States. The first maintains that Iran and the United States can reach a compromise based on mutual respect, noninterference in domestic affairs, and the advancement of shared interests. Those who hold this view acknowledge the animosity and historical grievances between the two countries but argue that it is possible to normalize their relations. The second school is more pessimistic. It deeply distrusts the United States and believes that Washington is neither ready nor committed to solving the disputes between the two countries.

Having worked within the Iranian government for nearly 30 years, and having sat on the secretariat of Iran's Supreme National Security Council for much of the decade before 2005, I was involved in discussions about both of these two approaches. My first personal experience in these matters dates to the late 1980s, when the critical issue facing the United States and Europe was the release of Western hostages in Lebanon. During that period, Iran received dozens of messages from Washington

HOSSEIN MOUSAVIAN is an associate research scholar at Princeton University and former spokesman for Iran's nuclear file.

proposing that each side, echoing U.S. President George H. W. Bush's 1989 inaugural address, show "goodwill for goodwill."

That year, Bush offered then Iranian President Ali Akbar Hashemi Rafsanjani a deal: If Iran assisted in securing the release of U.S. and Western hostages in Lebanon, the United States would respond with a gesture of its own. In response, Tehran emphasized its expectation that the United States would unfreeze and return billions of dollars in Iranian assets that were being held in the United States. The Iranian leadership also came away from discussions believing that Israel would reciprocate by releasing some Lebanese hostages, specifically Sheikh Abdul Karim Obeid, the leader of Hezbollah.

Then the two schools of thought came into play. Rafsanjani believed that this deal could be a confidence-building measure that would lead to rapprochement with the United States. Ayatollah Ali Khamenei, Iran's supreme leader, warned against trusting the United States and thought it naive to expect Washington to repay Tehran's efforts in kind. Then, as now, he believes that the United States is after nothing less in Iran than regime change. Ultimately, Iran decided to play a key role in securing the release of all Western hostages in Lebanon. But the United States neither released Iranian assets nor facilitated the release of Lebanese hostages.

Despite the affront, in subsequent years, Ayatollah Khamenei did not prevent Rafsanjani or, later, President Muhammad Khatami, from making more overtures to the West. In 1997, for example, Iran ratified the Chemical Weapons Convention, an agreement to decommission all chemical weapons by 2012. The same year, it also joined the Biological Weapons Convention. After 2001, Iran helped the United States oust the Taliban from much of Afghanistan, and for 20 consecutive months, between 2003 and 2005, it cooperated with the International Atomic Energy Agency. As the IAEA requested, the government opened various military facilities to inspections, suspended its enrichment activities, and implemented the Additional Protocol.

Although Iran expected that these gestures would open the way for it to continue a nuclear program (which it is authorized to do as a signatory of the Nuclear Nonproliferation Treaty), the United States and the West simply developed a new set of complaints against Iran. These included questions about Iran's nuclear-related program, its intentions toward Israel, and its hostility toward the U.S. military role in the region, particularly in Iraq and Afghanistan. Rather than reward Iran for cooperation, the United States implemented new sanctions and worked to increase international pressure on Tehran.

Ayatollah Khamenei was not surprised by Washington's behavior. Throughout this time, he routinely rejected direct talks with the United States aimed at a rapprochement. He argued that the United States wanted to negotiate from a position of strength; accordingly, it employed intimidation, pressure, and sanctions to bully Iran into submission. The West's increasingly hostile reactions to what Iran's leaders believed were moderate policies eventually gave the radicals the upper hand in domestic policies. And that ultimately led to the rise of Mahmoud Ahmadinejad.

Looking back, it is difficult to list all of the steps that each side might have taken to reverse the downward spiral in relations that followed. Certainly, the West, the United States in particular, missed great opportunities during the moderate presidencies of Rafsanjani and Khatami. More certainly, both sides would have needed a stronger commitment to changing the direction of U.S.-Iranian relations.

U.S. President Barack Obama's inauguration offered an opportunity for a new beginning. And once in office, he immediately signaled his willingness to enter into a dialogue with the Islamic Republic on a wide range of issues, aiming to remove 30 years of hostilities and create "constructive ties" between the two countries. In my view, even though the Iranian leadership was still skeptical about Obama's ability to break many long-standing U.S. policies, it believed in his personal intentions. For that reason, Iran's leaders decided to test the possibility of a breakthrough by granting a freer hand to Ahmadinejad in managing the relationship with Washington.

To be sure, much of Ahmadinejad's rhetoric about the relationship was harsh. But Iran made some unprecedented overtures as well. As Mohamed El Baradei, the former director of the IAEA, revealed in his memoir, Ahmadinejad sent a message in 2009 through him offering Obama a grand bargain. According to El Baradei, the Iranian president expressed a desire for direct talks with the United States, which would lead to bilateral negotiations, without preconditions. The talks would be held on the basis of mutual respect, and Iran would agree to help the United States in Afghanistan and elsewhere. Obama did not respond.

Almost all Westerners blame Tehran for the decline in relations since. They point to the failure of an initiative to swap Iran's highly enriched uranium for less-enriched fuel rods, which Russia and the United States proposed in Geneva in October 2009. A short time after that meeting, the Iranian government told El Baradei that Tehran would be willing to make the deal directly with the United States. Washington rejected the offer. Iran subsequently signed a similar agreement with Brazil and Turkey. That could have been an important confidence-building measure, but the United States rejected it, too.

In December 2010, the United States demonstrated for the first time a readiness to recognize Iran's legitimate right to enrich uranium for peaceful purposes. In an interview with the *BBC*, U.S. Secretary of State Hillary Clinton stated that Iran could enrich uranium once it demonstrated that it could do so in a responsible manner in accordance with its international obligations. In response, Iran made new overtures toward the United States. A reliable source told me that, during a February 2011 conference in Sweden, Iran's deputy foreign minister extended an official invitation to Marc Grossman, the U.S. special representative for Afghanistan and Pakistan, to visit Iran for talks on cooperation in Afghanistan. Washington dismissed the offer.

Then, in October 2011, Iran invited an IAEA team, led by Deputy Director General Herman Nackaerts, to visit the research-and-development sections of its heavy-water and centrifuge facilities. A contact told me that during the visit, Fereydoon Abbasi-Davani, the head of Iran's Atomic Energy Organization, offered a blank check to the IAEA, granting full transparency, openness to inspections, and cooperation with the IAEA. He also informed Nackaerts of Iran's receptiveness to putting the country's nuclear program under "full IAEA supervision," including implementing the Additional Protocol for five years, provided that sanctions against Iran were lifted.

Trying to make Iran's good intentions clearer, during a trip to New York in September 2011, Ahmadinejad announced that two American hikers who were being held in Iranian custody would be released. He signaled Iran's readiness to stop uranium enrichment to 20 percent if the United States gave the country fuel rods for the Tehran Research Reactor in return. This was an immensely important move to satisfy some of the West's demands and demonstrate that Iran is not seeking highly enriched uranium.

But the United States responded negatively again. Washington accused Tehran of plotting to assassinate the Saudi ambassador to the United States. It also influenced the substance and tone of the IAEA's November report on Iran by adding accusations of possible military dimensions to the country's nuclear program. Last month, Washington sanctioned the Central Bank of Iran; in effect, placed an oil embargo on the country; sponsored a UN resolution against Iran on terrorism; and orchestrated a UN resolution condemning Iran on human rights.

Explaining his Iran policy in New York in January, Obama proudly announced that he had mobilized the world and built an "unprecedented" sanctions regime targeting Iran. Obama said U.S.-led sanctions had reduced Iran's economy to "shambles." Three short years after the Obama administration introduced an engagement policy, Secretary of Defense Leon Panetta named Iran a "pariah state," reminding many of the previous administration's branding of Iran as part of the "axis of evil." Panetta noted that he hoped Obama's new policy would weaken the regime so that "they have to make a decision about whether they continue to be a pariah or whether they decide to join the international community."

These statements are clear evidence that Obama's engagement policy has failed. In fact, they support Ayatollah Khamenei's assessment that the core goal of U.S. policy is regime change. The door to rapprochement is closing. To keep it from slamming shut, the United States should declare, without condition, that it does not seek regime change in Tehran. Beyond that, the recognition of several principles is essential to bettering U.S.-Iranian relations after more than 30 bad years. For starters, both governments should practice patience and try to show mutual goodwill.

For one, both the United States and Iran are eager to understand the other's end game. Together, the two countries should draft a "grand agenda," which would include nuclear and all other bilateral, international, and regional issues to be discussed; outline what the ultimate goal will be; and describe what each side can gain by achieving it.

The United States and Iran should also work together on establishing security and stability in Afghanistan and preventing the Taliban's full return to power; securing and stabilizing Iraq; creating a Persian Gulf body to ensure regional stability; cooperating during accidents and emergencies at sea, ensuring freedom of navigation, and fighting piracy; encouraging development in Central Asia and the Caucasus; establishing a joint working group for combating the spread of weapons of mass destruction, terrorism; and eliminating weapons of mass destruction and drug trafficking in the Middle East. Finally, the two countries could do much good by strengthening the ties between their people through tourism, promoting academic and cultural exchanges, and facilitating visas.

It would be misguided for the United States to count on exploiting possible cleavages within the Iranian leadership. Iran's prominent politicians have their differences—like those in all countries—but they will be united against foreign interference and aggression. Both capitals should also progressively reduce threat-making, hostile behavior, and punitive measures during engagement to prove that they seek a healthier relationship. Engagement policy should be accompanied by actual positive actions, not just words.

I know enough about the dangers involved in the current direction of U.S. and Iranian policies to believe that change is essential. There is a peaceful path—one that will satisfy both Iranian and U.S. objectives while respecting Iran's legitimate nuclear rights. Washington and Tehran must find that right path together, and, despite what passes for debate in the international arena today, I believe they can.✸

Netanyahu's Iranian Dilemma

Letter From Tel Aviv

Ronen Bergman

ForeignAffairs.com, June 10, 2009

AT A recent symposium at Tel Aviv University, Major General Aharon Zeevi Farkash, the former chief of military intelligence, described Israel's public perception of the Iranian nuclear threat as "distorted." His view—which is shared by many in Israel's security and intelligence services—is that Israel is not Iran's primary target, and therefore, Israel must not attack Iran unilaterally. Members of the audience took issue with his analysis. One woman, speaking with a heavy Farsi accent, said of the Iranian regime, "They're crazy, and they will drop a bomb on us the moment they can. We need to deal with them now!"

Her sentiment reflects the public mood in Israel, where many are convinced that Iranian President Mahmoud Ahmadinejad wants to annihilate them and is willing to risk the destruction of his own country to do so. For most Israelis, the question is not whether Iran will attack but when. Polls consistently show that Israelis are overwhelmingly in favor of striking Iran's nuclear facilities. A recent survey commissioned by Tel Aviv University's Center for Iranian Studies found that three out of four Israelis believe the United States will not be able to stop Iran from acquiring nuclear weapons, and one in two supports taking immediate military action.

RONEN BERGMAN is a correspondent for the Israeli newspaper *Yedioth Ahronoth* and the author of *The Secret War With Iran*.

It is impossible to separate such convictions from their historical context. The fear that Jews—having escaped the furnaces of the Holocaust—could face annihilation in Israel has always haunted the public psyche. Long before Ahmadinejad's outbursts, therefore, Israelis were already attuned to hearing echoes of the Wannsee Conference in Tehran's inflammatory rhetoric. Historical comparisons between Tehran and Nazi-controlled Berlin are common, as is linking the Allied forces' refusal to bomb the concentration camps with the present international reluctance to take effective action against Iran. In April 2008, Benjamin Netanyahu, then leader of the opposition, made such an explicit comparison in a conversation with Stephen Hadley, then national security adviser in the Bush administration. "Ahmadinejad is a modern Hitler," Netanyahu told Hadley, "and the mistakes that were made prior to the Second World War must not be repeated."

But this visceral fear of Iran among the public and elected politicians is not shared by the intelligence community. Experts on the Iranian regime are quick to point out that Ahmadinejad does not call the shots in Iran; the real power lies with Ayatollah Ali Khamenei, the country's supreme religious leader. Furthermore, these experts note, throughout its 30 years of existence, the Iranian regime has shown pragmatism and moderation whenever its survival was at stake. And the Iranians clearly understand that a nuclear attack against Israel would lead to a devastating Israeli counterstrike that, among other things, would mean the end of the revolutionary regime. Finally, the Mossad and the Military Intelligence believe that the real reason the Iranians are intent on acquiring nuclear weapons—aside from the obvious considerations of prestige and influence—is to deter U.S. intervention and efforts at regime change.

Despite its assessment of Iran's motives, the Israeli intelligence community nonetheless believes that everything must be done to prevent Iran from becoming a nuclear power. To begin with, Israel cannot afford to risk nuclear weapons falling into the hands of someone less pragmatic than Khamenei; given its tiny size,

Israel would be unlikely to recover from even a single nuclear blast. This makes the risk of relying on the rationality of the Iranian regime intolerable. In addition, a nuclear Tehran could provide assistance to terror organizations—especially those active against Israel—without fear of reprisal. Lastly, an Iranian bomb would draw key regional players such as Egypt, Jordan, and Saudi Arabia into a regional nuclear arms race.

But ultimately, the intelligence community believes that Israel's military options are limited. No matter how great a success in tactical terms, even under the rosiest scenario, an air strike against Iran's nuclear installations would set its nuclear program back by only two or three years. Moreover, intelligence suggests that Iran would retaliate to such a strike by using its proxy forces—in particular, Hamas and Hezbollah—to unleash a wave of terrorist attacks against Israeli and Jewish targets around the world.

Israel's isolation on the question of Iran haunts both the public and the experts. If anything is to be done to thwart the nuclear ambitions of the regime in Tehran, Jerusalem will have to do so unilaterally—and bear the consequences. As Ariel Levite, the former deputy director general of the Israel Atomic Energy Commission, told a closed forum in April 2007, "The worst scenario of all would be if the president of the United States tells us: 'If you want to attack, then go ahead and attack. I won't stop you. But if you do attack, you will pay the price. It's up to you.'"

Israeli policymakers, then, are left to parse exactly how far President Barack Obama is willing to support Israel in its efforts to counter the Iranian threat. For the moment, Obama has made it clear that his focus is on talking with Iran. An Israeli attack would seriously undermine any hope of substantive dialogue. But the parameters of this dialogue are largely unknown, which makes Israel worried. Does the administration have clearly defined criteria for success? How will it decide that talks have failed, and how long will it tolerate a lack of progress? And perhaps the most worrisome question of all: Is a successful outcome of dialogue, as judged by Washington, compatible with Israel's security needs?

For now, Washington wants Israel to sit on its hands, and Israel has apparently agreed to do so. It is clear to all in Jerusalem that if Israel were to launch an unauthorized attack while the possibility of dialogue is still alive, the Obama administration might retaliate punitively, both diplomatically and economically. Indeed, some government officials in Jerusalem believe that any Israeli attack, even after diplomacy has failed, would require explicit American authorization.

Others, however, especially in Netanyahu's inner circle, believe that the statements made by members of the U.S. administration, including Obama himself, provide the wink and the nod that Israel needs in order to take action farther down the road. This, at least, is the impression that many in Jerusalem were left with after Netanyahu's visit to Washington last May, when neither Obama nor Secretary of Defense Robert Gates contradicted Netanyahu's assertion that Israel has a right to defend itself from an Iranian nuclear threat. The United States, Jerusalem believes, is actually pleased to see the Israeli military option on the table and is content to use it as leverage in future negotiations with Iran. The most direct U.S. request to hold off on any military action was made by CIA Director Leon Panetta on a trip to Israel just before Netanyahu's arrival in Washington—but, according to Israeli sources, he only referred to the next seven months. Israeli officials close to Netanyahu see only two conditions for future unilateral military action by Israel: that Jerusalem provide prior notification, and that it not ask Washington for an explicit *nihil obstat*.

Netanyahu himself still appears to be undecided. He has repeatedly stated over the years that Israel cannot countenance a nuclear Iran. In an interview I conducted with him in late 2007, he said: "We need to prepare for a situation in which we have failed and Iran has succeeded in acquiring a bomb. Against lunatics, deterrence must be absolute, total. The lunatics must understand that if they raise their hand against us, we will hit them in a way that will eviscerate any desire to harm us."

Some political analysts believe that this sort of language reflects Netanyahu's profound personal convictions and his sense of duty as a national leader. Others maintain that his tough-guy rhetoric is just a façade, part of his political persona. Netanyahu has probably learned from his highly controversial stint as prime minister in the 1990s. Fiascoes such as the failed 1997 attempt to assassinate the Hamas leader Khaled Mashal in Jordan humiliated Netanyahu and taught him that there are inherent dangers to wielding power. This, presumably, will make him think twice about sending the Israeli Air Force to Iran.

And yet campaign promises, if repeated often enough, have a tendency to create their own momentum. Public pressure to act is considerable. Netanyahu knows that a successful Iranian nuclear test could destroy his political future. Moreover, the immediate political environment in which Netanyahu operates is conducive to authorizing a preemptive strike. His senior coalition partner, Foreign Minister Avigdor Lieberman, has made threats against Iran on numerous occasions. And, unlike many of the country's mid-level intelligence analysts and security officials, the current leaders of the Mossad and the Shin Bet believe in solving problems by force.

As Iran approaches nuclear weapons capability—sometime in 2010, according to current Mossad estimates—an increasing number of people in Netanyahu's circle will adopt the view that Israel needs to take action and that the United States will be understanding of Israel's needs. And if the Obama administration is not so understanding? Israel may decide that the existential danger posed by a potential second Holocaust warrants risking even a serious rift with the United States. Ultimately, the fear of a nuclear-armed state whose leader talks openly of destroying Israel may outweigh the views of the country's intelligence experts. ☯

The Root of All Fears

Why Is Israel So Afraid of Iranian Nukes?

Ariel Ilan Roth

ForeignAffairs.com, November 24, 2009

THE SPECIAL relationship between Israel and the United States is about to enter perhaps its rockiest patch ever. Israel is growing exasperated with the Obama administration's effort to use diplomacy to roll back Iran's growing uranium-enrichment program. Israelis know better than anyone else that the trick to developing a nuclear weapon as a small power is to drag out the process of diplomacy and inspections long enough to produce sufficient quantities of fissionable material. Israel should know: in the 1960s, it deliberately misled U.S. inspectors and repeatedly delayed site visits, providing the time to construct its Dimona reactor and reprocess enough plutonium to build a bomb. North Korea has followed a similar path, with similar results. And now, Israel suspects, Iran is doing the same, only with highly enriched uranium instead of plutonium.

Most observers believe that Israel's preoccupation with Iran's nuclear program stems from the fear that Iran would either use a nuclear weapon against Israel or give the bomb to one of its direct proxies, most likely Hezbollah. Given Tehran's open hostility toward Jerusalem, such foreboding makes sense. But such a scenario is highly improbable.

ARIEL ILAN ROTH is the Associate Director of National Security Studies at the Johns Hopkins University's Krieger School of Arts and Sciences.

Tehran's profound dislike of the Jewish state notwithstanding, it is unlikely to attack Israel with a nuclear weapon because Israel's atomic arsenal is orders of magnitude larger than whatever infant capability Iran could muster in the foreseeable future. Moreover, Israel is believed to possess a secure submarine-based second-strike capability that could devastate Iran.

Nor would Iran readily supply Hezbollah with atomic weapons. No nuclear state has ever turned over its most prized military asset to a subsidiary actor or surrendered its exclusive control over a weapon that it worked so hard to obtain. More important, if Hezbollah were to acquire and use a nuclear weapon against Israel, there would be no doubt about the weapon's provenance and Iran would immediately face devastating retaliation. An attack on Israel, in other words, would mean the end of Iran.

Although many analysts question the rationality of the Iranian regime, it is in fact fairly conservative in its foreign policy. Iran has two long-range goals, achieving regional hegemony and spreading fundamentalist Islam, neither of which will be achieved if Iran initiates a nuclear exchange with Israel. Tehran's expanding influence in Iraq and the fear that it inspires in the Persian Gulf states are already advancing the first goal. Iran needs only to possess nuclear weapons, not to use them, in order to further enhance its international prestige and force adversaries to take it seriously. Likewise, the deterrent power of an unused nuclear capability would allow the regime to spread its ideology without the constant worry of regime change imposed from abroad.

Since it is doubtful that Iran will use nuclear weapons against Israel or surrender control of the ultimate weapon to Hezbollah—a point made recently by retired General Shlomo Gazit in Ma'arachot, the quarterly journal published by the Israeli military—one can safely assume that the root of Israel's Iranian obsession lies elsewhere.

Israel fears that Iran's nuclear ambitions could undermine its qualitative superiority of arms and its consistent ability to inflict disproportionate casualties on adversaries—the cornerstones of

Israel's defense strategy. Although some idealists dream of reconciliation in the Middle East based on a genuine and mutual recognition of all parties' legitimate rights, most Israelis believe the key to enduring peace in the Middle East is convincing Israel's adversaries that ejecting Israel through force is an impossible task not worth pursuing.

Essential to inducing that sense of despair is Israel's ability to continuously trounce its enemies on the battlefield and suffer far fewer losses than it inflicts. The Iranian nuclear program threatens Israel's ability to do this in two ways. First, an Iranian nuclear capability would likely force Israel to restrain itself due to fears that Iran's nuclear weapons could provide an implied security guarantee to other anti-Zionist forces—the sort of guarantee that would prevent Israel from causing the massive losses it has in the past, while giving anti-Israel forces the confidence to keep up the fight.

Israeli restraint during a war could take many forms, but it is unlikely that the unmitigated rout of the 1967 Six-Day War or the direct threat posed to Arab capitals at the end of the 1973 Yom Kippur War would have occurred if a nuclear guarantee had been forthcoming from a true regional adversary such as Iran, rather than from a distant superpower such as the Soviet Union, whose chief interest lay in the humiliation of its rival, not the destruction of Israel.

The even greater threat posed by Iran's nuclear program is its potential to unleash a cascade of proliferation in the Middle East, beginning with Egypt and Saudi Arabia. For both of these states, the idea that Jews and Persians could have a monopoly on nuclear weapons in a region demographically and culturally dominated by Arabs is shameful. For Saudi Arabia, a security motivation will be at play as well, given its physical proximity to Iran and the strategic imperative of deterring any Iranian threat to Saudi Arabia's oil-production facilities.

The development of nuclear weapons by Egypt or Saudi Arabia would pose a grave danger to the Jewish state, despite the fact that Egypt has signed a peace treaty with Israel. This is because leaders who have reconciled themselves to Israel's existence—including those of Egypt, Jordan, and certain segments of the Palestinian national movement—have done so because they believed Israel was strong but unlikely to endure in the long term. (Egyptian President Anwar Sadat, for example, justified his pursuit of a peace process with Israel by comparing the Israelis to crusaders: strong today, gone tomorrow.) More broadly, as the Palestinian-American political scientist Hilal Khashan's work on Arab attitudes toward peace has shown, the willingness of Arabs to make peace with Israel is a direct function of their perception of Israel's invincibility. Just as an Iranian nuclear capability would imply a nuclear guarantee for anti-Zionist proxies, an Egyptian or Saudi nuclear capability would reduce incentives for other Arab states to make peace with Israel because, shielded under an Arab nuclear umbrella, they would no longer fear catastrophic defeat or further loss of territory.

Such developments would shatter the perception of Israeli invincibility on which successive Israeli governments have pinned their hopes for eventual peace in the region. As a result, Israel's security would be dependent on maintaining a state of perpetual armed readiness and hair-trigger alert that could counter immediate threats but only in an inconclusive manner, as displayed recently in Lebanon and Gaza. The restraint that Israel showed in both conflicts out of deference to U.S. and European concerns would only be magnified by the new fear of crossing an Arab red line. Future operations resembling the 2006 invasion of Lebanon or the January 2009 attack on Gaza are likely to be even more restrained and therefore, by Israel's own metric, less effective in pushing Arabs toward peace. In fact, such operations may do Israel more harm than good, because as Israel uses less force and causes less damage, the deterrent effect that Israel hopes to bolster through such operations only gets further eroded.

The possibility that Israel may no longer be capable of forcing peace upon those who deny its right to exist is beginning to dawn on many Israelis. Whether Israel attacks Iran's nuclear infrastructure or not, the time has come for Israel's defense community to develop a strategic doctrine for long-term coexistence that does not rely on a posture of invincibility. But, given that widespread Arab acceptance of Israel's right to exist does not appear to be on the horizon, most Israelis, including the current prime minister, insist that Israel's most urgent strategic objective is to stop Iran from developing a nuclear weapon. Doing so would temporarily remove the threat of a regional nuclear cascade and maintain Israel's superiority of arms. More important, it would hold at bay the suspicion that Israel may never attain true peace. This increasingly widespread fear has a toxic effect on national morale, is an existential threat to the Jewish state, and lies at the root of Israel's obsession with the Iranian bomb.✪

What Happens After Israel Attacks Iran

Public Debate Can Prevent a Strategic Disaster

Ehud Eiran

ForeignAffairs.com, February 23, 2012

SINCE ITS birth in 1948, Israel has launched numerous preemptive military strikes against its foes. In 1981 and 2007, it destroyed the nuclear reactors of Iraq and Syria, operations that did not lead to war. But now, Israelis are discussing the possibility of another preemptive attack—against Iran—that might result in a wider conflict.

The public debate in Israel about whether Jerusalem should order a strike on Iran's nuclear program is surprisingly frank. Politicians and policymakers often discuss the merits of an attack in public; over the past year, for example, Israeli Prime Minister Benjamin Netanyahu and Defense Minister Ehud Barak have sparred regularly and openly with former Mossad director Meir Dagan, the most prominent opponent of an Israeli operation. But much of the conversation is focused on whether Israel should

EHUD EIRAN is a Postdoctoral Fellow at the Department of International Relations at the University of Haifa in Israel and a faculty affiliate of the Middle East Negotiation Initiative at the Program on Negotiation at Harvard Law School. He is a former Israeli government official and a former research fellow at Harvard's Belfer Center for Science and International Affairs.

strike, not on what might happen if it does—in other words, the result on the "day after."

Indeed, the analysis in Israel about the possible effects of a bombing campaign against Iran is limited to a small, professional elite, mostly in government and behind closed doors. This intimate circle that does consider scenarios of the "day after" concentrates almost exclusively on what an Iranian response, direct or through proxies, might look like. This is not surprising, given that Israel must worry first and foremost about the immediate military implications of an Iranian counterattack. But in doing so, Israeli policymakers are ignoring several of the potential longer-term aspects of a strike: the preparedness of Israel's home front; the contours of an Israeli exit strategy; the impact on U.S.-Israeli relations; the global diplomatic fallout; the stability of world energy markets; and the outcome within Iran itself. Should Israel fail to openly debate and account for these factors in advance of an attack, it may end up with a strategic debacle, even if it achieves its narrow military goals.

Israeli officials have thought extensively about how the first moves of a military conflict between Jerusalem and Tehran might play out. Ephraim Kam, a former Israeli military intelligence officer and deputy head of Israel's Institute for National Security Studies (INSS), reflected the general consensus in the security establishment when he wrote in the Institute's 2010 strategic assessment that Iran may respond in two possible ways to an Israeli operation: missile strikes on Israel, either directly or through allied organizations such as Hezbollah or Hamas; or terror attacks, likely on Israeli targets abroad by Iranians or those proxy groups.

A direct Iranian response would involve a missile barrage from Iran onto Israeli territory, similar to the volley of rockets launched at Israel by Iraq during the first Gulf War. Only one Israeli citizen died then, and it seems that Israeli officials estimate that the damage of a similar Iranian strike would be greater, but still limited. This past November, Ehud Barak, referring to possible direct and proxy-based Iranian retaliation, said that "There is no scenario for 50,000 dead, or 5,000 killed—and if everyone stays in their homes, maybe not even 500 dead." Barak's calm also reflects Israel's previous experience in preempting nuclear threats. Iraq did not respond when Israel destroyed its nuclear facility in 1981, disproving the doomsday predictions made by several Israeli experts prior to the strike, and Syria remained silent when Israel bombed its nascent reactor in 2007.

Israeli policymakers also do not seem particularly concerned about the prospect of a proxy response. They recognize that Hezbollah, as it did in 2006, can target Israel with a large number of rockets. Yet in an interview with Ronen Bergman in *The New York Times* late last month, several Israeli experts argued that, regardless of a potential battle with Iran, the probability of an extended conflict with Hezbollah is already high. According to this logic, an attack on Iran would merely hasten the inevitable and might actually be easier to sustain before, not after, Iran acquires nuclear weapons. In addition, the new constraints now operating against Hezbollah—the ongoing revolt in Syria chief among them—might even limit the ability of the organization to harm Israel in a future conflict. Indeed, over the past several months, the Secretary General of Hezbollah, Sheikh Hassan Nasrallah, has emphasized the group's independence, saying on February 7 that "the Iranian leadership will not ask Hezbollah to do anything. On [the day of an Israeli attack on Iran], we will sit, think, and decide what we will do."

Meanwhile, the Israeli security establishment remains confident that Iran and its proxies will have trouble staging large-scale attacks on Israeli or Jewish targets abroad. Iran and Hezbollah have done so successfully in the past, most notably in response to Israel's assassination, in 1992, of Hezbollah's first secretary general (they are strongly suspected to have directed suicide bombings against the Israeli embassy and the Jewish community center in Buenos Aires in 1992 and 1994, respectively). Israeli experts such as Kam agree that similar attacks could occur again in the wake of a strike on Iran, but argue that Tehran's ability to respond is limited, likely due to its own handicaps and the restrictions posed by the post-9/11 global effort against terrorism. They gained support for their theory in mid-February, when, according to preliminary evidence, Iranian agents staged clumsy, botched attacks on Israeli targets in Georgia, India, and Thailand, injuring only one person in New Delhi and ending in humiliation in Bangkok, with one operative accidentally blowing off his legs.

Balanced against these threats is the expected benefit of an Israeli bombing campaign. According to Bergman, the Israeli defense community estimates that it can inflict a three-to-five-year delay on the Iranian nuclear project. But in its optimistic estimation about the success of an attack and about Israel's ability to deter any response, it has failed to address, at least publicly, several crucial factors.

Although Israel has buttressed its home-front preparedness since its 2006 war with Hezbollah, it seems that it must do much more to ready the country for the rocket and missile attacks that it is expected to endure after a strike against Iran's nuclear program. In a move that Israelis are now sardonically mocking, the former minister for home front defense, Matan Vilnai, left his post in February to become Israel's ambassador to China. Before departing, Vilnai staged an angry outburst during a Knesset subcommittee meeting on February 7 over the lack of homeland preparedness, creating such a stir that the chairman had to end the meeting. Data presented at the session reveal the source of Vilnai's frustration: a quarter of all Israelis do not have the most basic physical shelter needed to weather sustained rocket fire. Gas masks, a basic safety measure against a chemical attack, are available to only 60 percent of the population. And Vilnai's former ministry lacks the bureaucratic muscle to win the resources and funds necessary to improve the situation. When the Netanyahu administration established the ministry early last year, the Israeli journalist Ofer Shelah called it "the big lie" because it "has no authority, no independent budget, and no ability to affect national priorities."

The lack of readiness within Israel is all the more worrisome in light of the fact that Israeli analysts have spent little time discussing an exit strategy. An Israeli strike might follow a version of the previous attacks against the Iraqi and Syrian nuclear programs, which did not lead to conflict. Or, following the example of Israel's 1982 invasion of Lebanon, it might spark a prolonged war. That operation, intended to remove the threat of armed Palestinian groups within two days, instead lasted 18 years, and contributed to the evolution of a new enemy in Hezbollah. Similarly, Israel's incursion into Lebanon in 2006 had no clear exit strategy and lasted an unexpected 33 days, ending in confusion. Without serious public discussion about the possibility of a long war with Iran, Israel could enter an extended conflict unprepared to provide for and defend its citizens.

Israeli leaders have also failed to address in public the effect of an Israeli strike on U.S.-Israeli relations. There is, of course, much conversation about whether the United States and Israel agree on the need for a strike, and, if so, when it should occur. So far, it seems, Jerusalem and Washington remain united in their opposition to Iran's nuclear program, but are not yet in agreement about the time for military action; indeed, Israel has refused to commit to warning Washington in advance of an attack. Should Israel bomb Iran, it could easily provoke a crisis even if it did first warn the United States, especially if the Obama administration has to intervene. Once again, Israeli strategic thinking on the issue is likely informed by the 1981 bombing of Iraq's nuclear reactor. The attack infuriated the White House, which condemned it and, in punishment, suspended the delivery of some aircraft to Israel. Yet Washington retroactively approved of the strike and restored and even strengthened its relationship with Jerusalem—a process that Netanyahu may expect to repeat itself. The prime minister might also be calculating that, in an election year, Obama would prefer to avoid openly criticizing Israel after an attack.

In addition, the broader diplomatic impact of an Israeli strike has also received little open attention. The former Mossad director

Meir Dagan has raised the possibility that an attack might disrupt the existing international pressure on Iran, which is now beginning to place severe strain on the regime, and make it harder for that coalition to re-form in the event that Iran restarts its program. On the whole, however, Israeli leaders have not confronted that possibility, seeming to place faith in the efficacy of the three-to-five-year delay that they hope a strike will achieve.

Also largely missing from Israel's public analysis is the question of how a bombing campaign would affect worldwide energy markets. As a small country with a limited global perspective, Israel rarely needs to consider the international impact of its actions. The few Israeli analysts who have looked into this question have tended to underplay Iran's intention, and capability, of acting on its threat to close the Strait of Hormuz. Last month, for example, Amos Yadlin, the former director of Israel's military intelligence, and Yoel Guzansky, the former head of the Iran desk of Israel's national security council, argued in a paper for the INSS that it is highly doubtful that Iran would block the waterway.

That lack of perspective extends to what might happen inside of Iran after a strike. The public discourse about an attack rarely includes any consideration of whether a bombing campaign would galvanize Iranians to rally around the current leadership, ruining any chance of the regime change that might ultimately be necessary to end the threat of a nuclear program. Israel remains unwilling to estimate whether a strike would hurt or help the cause of the dissidents; its failure to predict the Arab Spring has humbled its proclivity for making such forecasts.

And so there is a gap in Israel's debate about Iran. Although Israeli experts focus heavily on the immediate implications of the "day after," they neglect, with a few exceptions, the broader repercussions of an attack. Ironically, then, at the core of the elite, scientific calculations regarding an attack on Iran and its aftermath stands a certain kind of fatalism. It is based on the traditional trust that Israelis place in their leaders, and on their sense that open conversation might in fact harm Israeli interests. But the lack of public debate may, in the event of an attack, leave Israel handicapped both in its ability to strike and to defend itself.

In particular, a lack of open discussion leaves the Israel Defense Forces as the primary source of information and analysis on a strike. The IDF, given its narrow focus on the military aspects of an attack, may fail to fully consider its potential political and diplomatic impact. A more public debate might strengthen those in the bureaucracy who are urging the Israeli government to weigh those other factors as carefully as the military planning. The elevation of those voices could then prevent Israeli leaders from operating on the basis of limited information and faulty assumptions. If history is any guide, Israeli policymakers could benefit from such an expansion of the conversation. Israel's disastrous invasion of Lebanon in 1982 began with a war plan that the public had not vetted. The operation ended after overwhelming pressure from civil society, a process that took nearly two decades. To avoid a similar strategic blunder in confronting Iran's nuclear program—either as a result of an attack, or a failure to do so—Israel should give the public a stake in the debate about the "day after" much sooner than that.⊛

Why Israel Should Learn to Stop Worrying and Love the Bomb

The Case for a New Nuclear Strategy

Dmitry Adamsky

ForeignAffairs.com, March 31, 2012

THE DEBATE over Iran's nuclear program has made clear that when it comes to nuclear deterrence, Israeli strategic thinking is flawed. In the 1960s, Israel developed a nuclear capability as the ultimate security guarantee, a last resort to be used if the country's very existence was threatened. This capability became popularly known as the "Samson Option," after the Jewish biblical hero who, rather than face death alone, brought down the roof of a Philistine temple, killing both himself and his enemies. At the same time, Israeli strategy has been guided by a belief that any adversary developing weapons of mass destruction is an existential threat that must be stopped. This belief came to be known as the Begin Doctrine, after Prime Minister Menachem Begin used force to stop the Iraqi nuclear program in 1981.

This leads to a paradox: the basic potential advantage of the "Samson Option" is that it could deter a nuclear-armed foe. But the Begin Doctrine prevents Israel from benefiting from the "Samson Option," as it seeks to ensure that the situation in which a nuclear capability would be most useful will never come to pass.

DMITRY ADAMSKY is assistant professor at the Lauder School of Government, Diplomacy, and Strategy at the Interdisciplinary Center Herzliya and the author of *The Culture of Military Innovation*.

Today, the majority of Israel's strategists promote some kind of a preventive attack on Iran, as they do not believe a nuclear-armed Iran could be deterred and reject the notion of stability based on mutual assured destruction (MAD). Some suggest that Iranian leaders, driven by messianic religious ideology, would use their weapons to destroy Israel, regardless of the costs. Others argue that even if Iranian decision-makers were rational, Iran's conspiratorial worldview and lack of direct communications with Jerusalem could lead Tehran to misread Israeli signals and to miscalculate, triggering unintended nuclear escalation. Another common argument against MAD is that Iran's acquisition of a nuclear weapon would result in a dangerous proliferation cascade across the Middle East.

But these attitudes obscure the real reason that Israel refuses to live with an Iranian bomb. Israel's intolerance of MAD is not limited to any particular adversary or set of circumstances, but, rather, derives from its paradoxical nuclear strategy. The "Samson Option" is by nature an asymmetrical deterrence model: Israel seeks to deter without being deterred.

Maintaining asymmetrical deterrence would be impossible if Iran did ultimately develop a nuclear weapon. But Israel need not see that outcome as the end of the world. If anything, deterring a nuclear-armed adversary is exactly what Israel's nuclear capability is good for. But in order to make the best use of its "Samson Option," Israel needs to start thinking about and publicly debating how it would position itself against a nuclear-armed Iran. In short, Israel needs a new nuclear strategy.

WHAT IS IT GOOD FOR?

FOR MOST countries, the primary goal of nuclear weapons is to deter their use by others. But Israel's "Samson Option" has nothing to do with the nuclear balance of terror. The balance of terror, known to most strategists as an unavoidable evil of the atomic age, is seen in Israel not as a strategic challenge but as a materialized, existential, and unacceptable threat. Although the "Samson Option" hypothetically enables MAD, Israeli leaders will have nothing of it. The development of nuclear capabilities by an adversary is a casus belli and demands immediate diplomatic, clandestine, or military preemption. This explains why Israel launched airstrikes on Iraq in 1981 and, reportedly, on Syria in 2007 in order to secure its nuclear monopoly.

Instead, Israel's nuclear program was allegedly devised to serve as an ultimate guarantor against a doomsday scenario in which an all-out conventional attack by a coalition of enemies threatened the total annihilation of the state. But it is not clear that Israel's nuclear deterrent has had any bearing on the strategic calculus of its foes during past wars. It did not deter the Egyptians and Syrians from invading Israel in 1973, Iraq from launching missiles on Israel in 1991, the Palestinians from turning to violence during two intifadas, or Hezbollah and Hamas from raining rockets on Israel during the last decade. None of these attacks were kept at bay by a balance of military force that overwhelmingly favored Israel.

To be sure, a nuclear capability would be hypothetically useful if Israel's conventional qualitative military edge were completely eroded, leaving only a nuclear last resort. But such a scenario is unlikely; the raison d'être of Israel's national security policy is to retain conventional superiority, and the country is constantly building up its forces toward this goal. Furthermore, at least for the foreseeable future, the United States will continue to guarantee Israel's military edge.

So if MAD is not an option, and Israel can deter conventional threats with conventional forces, then what is the "Samson Option" good for? It seems that Israel derives no concrete benefits from its nuclear capability. To understand, then, why Israel produced a nuclear capability and crafted a deterrence strategy for a scenario that it cannot tolerate, one has to look at Israel's unique strategic culture.

Unlike other countries, Israel did not undertake its nuclear project because of geostrategic aspirations, a desire for prestige, or to defend against nuclear adversaries. Even in the late 1950s, when the project was conceived as a so-called great equalizer against larger Arab militaries, Israel's conventional might was already seen as the main countermeasure against its neighbors. When Israel reportedly crossed the nuclear threshold in 1967, the conventional power of the Israeli army was at its peak, leaving no doubt to Israelis that it could effectively deter its opponents in the future.

For Israelis, security practices and military innovations are usually not driven by strategic theory but by ad-hoc solutions to burning problems and by creative improvisations. As the historian Avner Cohen showed in *The Worst-Kept Secret*, Israel's nuclear project was initiated without a careful analysis of the long-term strategic objectives, applications, and implications of this new capability. With little political guidance, the Israelis at first focused only on building infrastructure and capabilities, and avoided articulating complex issues of nuclear doctrine.

More than for any perceived security benefits, Israel's nuclear project was conceived for psychological comfort in face of the unthinkable quintessence of all Jewish and Israeli fears: a second Holocaust. For millennia, life in the diaspora was an uninterrupted struggle for survival. Enslavement, persecution, and systematic annihilation have had a profound impact on the Israeli approach to national security. This fundamental sense of insecurity, a siege mentality that results in the assumption that the country is under a constant existential threat, predisposes Jerusalem to seek absolute security. At the core of Israeli strategy rests the notion that the country can survive and politically engage its neighbors only from a position of military superiority; symmetry in conventional and nuclear affairs is unthinkable.

GETTING MAD

A NUMBER of thinkers, including former U.S. National Security Adviser Zbigniew Brzezinski, argue that because the "Samson Option" offers it few tangible benefits, Israel should give up its nuclear project in exchange for Iran doing the same. But this argument overlooks Israel's strategic mentality. Without understanding Israeli strategic culture, foreign observers cannot fully grasp just how profound the psychological barriers are that Israel must surmount in order to think systematically about how to live with and deter a nuclear-armed Iran.

Given that Israel's nuclear capability exists to calm the dread of perceived existential threats, Jerusalem would accept nuclear disarmament only as a consequence of a regional peace agreement and normalization, not as a prelude to them. Any other solution would be seen as premature and counterproductive. This approach to disarmament, coupled with an aversion to consider MAD, has put Israel in a strategic bind with regard to Iran.

Whether Israel can stop Iran from getting the bomb is the question of the day. But if, for whatever reason, the Begin Doctrine fails, the far more important question looming on the horizon is how to live with a nuclear Iran. Israel's security elite is inclined to believe that the end of the country's regional nuclear monopoly—brought on by an Iranian nuclear weapon—would leave it defenseless and vulnerable to total annihilation. But Iran's developing a nuclear bomb would discredit only the Begin Doctrine, not the "Samson Option." And in that case, Israel would need to embrace its "Samson Option" and adjust its strategy to derive the most tangible benefits from it.

To begin with, Israel should consider outlining its nuclear posture to enhance strategic stability and assure Israelis that their government could successfully deter a nuclear Iran. This would entail communicating its redlines and how it would respond if Iran crossed them. Israel may be uninterested in full disclosure so as to avoid international pressure to disarm. But Jerusalem can find a way to outline a general doctrine without revealing specific capabilities. An ambiguous posture alone might not be enough to ensure stable deterrence, but a full disclosure could be provocative.

Israeli strategists would also have to explore the relationship between conventional and nuclear deterrence and examine whether the Israel Defense Forces could deter a nuclear-armed Iran more credibly with its conventional might. The optimal balance between deterrence by denial (using defensive measures to limit the effectiveness of an enemy strike) and deterrence by punishment (threatening a heavy offensive retaliation to any attack) should be found and communicated to Iran. Both Israel and Iran would need to introduce a vocabulary of MAD so that each side understood the rules of the game. And to avoid any nuclear miscalculation, each side would need to carefully study the other's strategic culture.

Today, Israel's deterrence strategy, like its other strategies, is not a written doctrine but a vague, tacit concept. Any causality between Israel's actions and its adversaries' behavior is more assumed than proven. Israel lacks an institution charged with verifying the effectiveness of its deterrence. Jerusalem cannot afford this in the nuclear age—significant intellectual and organizational energy should be invested in formulating, managing, and evaluating deterrence policy on the national level.

Finally, if Iran gets the bomb, Israel will have to overcome several deeply ingrained beliefs before it can make the necessary adjustments to its deterrence strategy. Israel would need to accept the irony of its security stemming from the constant threat of annihilation. This would entail a fundamental departure from Israel's habit of seeing absolute military superiority as the key to its stability. Israel's government would also have to learn to see Iran in a different light. Viewing Iran as a reasonable, if radical, actor would be a jarring departure from earlier beliefs, but it would be a necessary precondition to any kind of interaction between the two countries. Seeing Iran's leaders as religiously motivated fanatics could lead to a nuclear war.

Israel has sworn to prevent Iran from becoming a nuclear-armed state, but has not prepared for what happens if it does. So far, Israel's policymakers have avoided publicly exploring strategies for coping with a nuclear-armed Iran out of fear that talking about the issue would compromise Israel's nuclear opacity and communicate Israel's acceptance of an Iranian nuclear weapon. But public debate could generate insights on how to establish stable deterrence and avoid dangerous escalation. It could help Israel overcome the cognitive dissonances of its nuclear strategy, and, in making Tehran familiar with the Israeli mind-set, minimize the chances of miscalculation. This debate should start now, because the cost of waiting until the morning after Iran has a nuclear weapon, if it does in fact acquire one, is too great.

Acknowledgements

This book would not have appeared without the talent, judgment, and hard work of the *Foreign Affairs* staff: from Editorial, Andrew Bast, Stuart Reid, Justin Vogt, Benjamin Alter, Edward Fishman, Sigrid von Wendel, Lorenz Skeeter, Ann Tappert, Belinda Lanks, Sarah Larson, Sarah Foster, and Elira Coja; from Publishing, Lynda Hammes, Emilie Harkin, Christine Leonard, Ed Walsh, Michael Pasuit, Jonathan Chung, Carolina Aguilar, Daniel Schoenbaechler, and Katie Sedgwick; and from Communications, David Mikhail. Associate Editor Katie Allawala played the largest role, expertly shepherding the project from start to finish. Here and in the magazine in general, their efforts consistently rise to the level of the subject matter they deal with, which is all that needs to be said.

Gideon Rose
Editor, *Foreign Affairs*

Jonathan Tepperman
Managing Editor, *Foreign Affairs*

August 2012

17606534R00109

Made in the USA
Lexington, KY
19 September 2012